THE FOUNDATION OF HONOR

PAULO VENTURA

TSM PUBLISHING
530 BROAWAY, 3ᴿᴰ FL
LAWRENCE, MA 01841

Copyright © 2020 by Dr. Terika T. Smith/Terika Smith Ministries

All rights reserved. No part of this book may be reproduced in any form without the permission in writing from the publisher, except in the case of brief quotations embodied in critical articles or reviews.

All scripture quotation unless otherwise indicated are taken from The Holy Bible, New Living Translation1996 and King James Version, 1960. Used by permission. All rights reserved.

Designed by RichWired

Manufactured in the United States of America

For any ordering information or special discounts for bulk purchases, please contact us @ terika5021@gmail.com

Published in the United States by TSM Publishing
ISBN # 978-0-9965967-8-7
Library of Congress # 2020931419

Gratitude

My thanks to all those who walk with me daily in ministry. First, my wife Cosma, who endures my absences as I travel to minister. My daughters Raquel, Marcia, Alice and Ana Paula who cover me daily with prayers and care.

To the ministers who opened the doors to bring this precious theme to their churches, resulting in growth and many blessings.

To all of them I am grateful for their love and companionship. The Lord will reward you.

But the honor and glory for the production of this work go only to one: To Him who is the only one worthy of receiving glory and honor. Without Him none of this would have been possible. I depended entirely on Him to write these lines. I praise Him every day for helping relieve my tiredness, bringing powerful revelations, surrounding me with tranquility to write and, above all, bringing the indispensable inspiration for me to reach the end.

To you, my beloved, faithful, kind and generous Lord, my Eternal Father, my King and my Savior I give all praise, worship, glory, and honor. On my knees I say, Thank you very much.

Paul Ventura

Preface

In these last days, God is restoring the Church to having a Kingdom Mentality. Churches who are in tune with the kingdom mindset and who manage to assimilate in their spirit these connections will understand how to operate within the Government of God.

This restored Mentality passes through the rescue of one of the greatest teachings of Master Jesus Christ to His apostles, disciples, and followers, that is, His Church: The Foundation of the Kingdom.

In Ephesians 2:20 NKJV the Apostle Paul releases a code for the Church when he writes:

> *having been built on the foundation of the apostles and prophets, Jesus Christ Himself being the chief cornerstone.*

The big question is, what are these apostolic and prophetic foundations taught by the Messiah? Are they described in the Holy Scriptures or were they lost over time?
In this powerful book full of revelations, Paul Ventura will share with us one of these teachings of Jesus that will change our worldview in relation to our Christian lifestyle: The Foundation of Honor.

The Foundation of Honor will bring birth to a Culture of Honor in us and in future generations, shredding our leadership structure as we know it and presenting an expanded vision of the Body of Christ.

The Church needs to live a radical change. Relearning these fundamentals and living them is a great challenge. This book will bring a renewal in our mind and motivation necessary for the practice of these divine teachings.

I joyfully appreciated the ideas and concepts published here in this book. The author was deep in some respects, showing the richness of the man who decides to live in honor.

I hope that all those who are pleased to meditate on these lines will discover the best of spiritual life as long as we live on this earth.

Honor is the way of blessing. Honor is the way to victory.
I congratulate my friend Paulo Ventura on this jewel that he puts in our hands.

Apostle Lisdervan Portella

Foreword
By Apostle, Dr. Terika Smith

The book, The Foundation of Honor, by Apostle Paulo Ventura is a must read by every individual especially those involved in ministry. Whether it is the ministry of parenting, the ministry of government or the ministry of leadership within the realm of the church, *The Foundation of Honor* speaks to walking in God's perfect design on Honor. It takes the reader from honor to dishonor to restored honor. The book takes care with using the word of God as the road map along this journey and in this simplest of formats where anyone can engage in the reading and walk away having learned the material.

I am intrigued by the way Apostle Ventura highlights the origin of honor, when honor shifted to dishonor and how honor is restored. I am also intrigued by the care taken in broadening the reach span from the church world to every aspect of our lives. The way he discussed honor in the life of Eli and his sons. Not only was Eli a father, but he was also the judge and High Priest. Today, we do not stop to think that honor has different layers and it is important to not meet the requisites in one spectrum and miss it in the others.

Apostle Ventura leaves a strong sense of conviction in the heart of the reader to delve deeper in to their own personal, professional and ministerial lives and consider where or how they align with God's divine plan on honor.

This book is excellent for ministries that are looking to build a team, a home, a government on Godly principles. I highly recommend it as a must read for everyone serving in the role of pastor, armorbearer, mentor, or leader.

Apostle, Dr. Terika Smith

Presentation

Once again, we are surprised by the presentation of a special work by the Apostle Paul Ventura. This time brings to light a book that deeply immerses us in one of the foundations of the Kingdom of God.

The subject is treated in such a way that even the latest of Bible readers will understand why the Kingdom of God is supported by eternal foundations. The writer did not use technical, scholarly and difficult-to-understand theological language. He used, as always, a colloquial language, without lowering the quality level of his vocabulary to make himself understood in an easy and pleasant way.

There are points that reveal to us that the research done was oriented to search for and reveal the densest secrets hidden by Biblical languages and traditional Jewish culture.

Honor is one of the eternal foundations that were established by the Lord before the foundation of the world. Unfortunately, many Christians are not interested in the riches that the Word of God shows us, and therefore, even if converted, and saved, they do not project themselves into the wonders that this Word contains for our building and our knowledge of the things of God.

The writer was very happy in his approach to this subject. There are not that many people that dare to minister on topics that challenge our understanding, to understand the desired and planned way of life for each of us.

It is not enough to be a Christian, and lead a mediocre life without living the abundance of which the Lord Jesus told us, when in one of His famous sermons he said,

The thief does not come except to steal, and to kill, and to destroy. I have come that they may have life, and that they may have it more abundantly.
John 10:10 NKJV

The thief, to whom our King and Master referred o, is not the devil, as many proclaim out there. A more accurate examination of the original text, with good exegesis, reveals to us that the thief mentioned there are false teachers who misrepresent the Word and teach false doctrine to the Lord's disciples.

They are thieves of God's knowledge. They make God's children live in ignorance, so that they do not have access to the treasures that the Lord only reveals to those who seek to know Him through His own Word.

One day, the Lord complained that His people were perishing, that is right, dying for lack of knowledge. The Lord never complained about the lack of prayer, lack of praise, lack of fasting, and other religious activities that believer's practice. But from knowledge that is fundamental, for those who wish to grow in understanding divine actions, He complained.

We congratulate the Apostle Paul Ventura, who was not intimidated by the challenge of presenting us with this publication, which leads us to meditate very seriously and focused on the practice of honor among God's people.

His reflections are strong. We are sure that reading this book will lead many readers to rethink their way of life in the presence of the Eternal. Living in honor is God's will for us. Good reading to everyone.

The Editors

Index

GRATITUDE 4

PREFACE 6

FOREWORD 8

PRESENTATION 10

CHAPTER 01 16

CHAPTER 2 36

CHAPTER 3 68

CHAPTER 4 86

CHAPTER 5 98

CHAPTER 6 120

CHAPTER 7 136

CHAPTER 8 154

ABOUT THE AUTHOR 182

BIBLIOGRAPHY 184

NOTES 186

Chapter 01

THE FIRST ADAM
FROM HONOR TO DISHONOR
Introduction

In creating man and placing him in the Garden of Eden, the Lord planned for man to reign on this earth, giving him special treatment, and using His own image as a model for this creature placed in this new world that He had begun.

The divine idea was to project the divine Kingdom on earth. Hence why he created man from the earth itself, that he may assume the entire earthly government, following the guidance and orders of the celestial Kingdom. He, the Lord, was handing over into man's hands a kingdom so that he might develop it and rule upon such kingdom.

As the model of the Kingdom was the same as heaven, man received divine plans, from which came all the foundations for this kingdom to be divine and to sustain himself in these eternal foundations, among which honor was included.
Man's honorable mission was only to reproduce the celestial model in the dimension of light and matter. God wanted to see and admire His will expressed on earth, through a people created by himself man, who had been His masterpiece in the creation of this new world.

When created, man was awarded with virtues inherent to the Lord, because, in addition to the image, God also wanted man to bear His likeness, that is, that he would look like Him in every sense of the word.

What is man that You are mindful of him,
And the son of man that You visit him?
5 For You have made him a little lower than the angels,
And You have crowned him with glory and honor.
Psalm 8:4-5

See that the Lord covered him with honor and glory, because the mission that would be given to man was a noble office. The nobility only operates in honor and glory.

Certainly, the desire of the Most High was not to establish a Church on earth. He wasn't worried or interested in religious services. He did not give a Church to man; He delivered a kingdom. And God put him as the government of this kingdom. When man was confronted with the temptation of sin and gave in, he did not lose his salvation, he lost an entire Kingdom. He was stripped of his aptitude to lead a kingdom. There was a disconnect from his divine source. The earth leader became disconnected from the Supreme King and that's why man lost glory and honor.

We need to understand the principle so as not to miss the end In the beginning, it all began the inauguration of the celestial kingdom on Earth. After man's fall, he entered an unceasing and cruel battle to try to win back this kingdom. Despite the advances, the comings and goings, of some victories and many other defeats, and of the constant divine help, man did not succeed.

The Lord had already prophesied that the woman's seed would crush the serpent's head, so the day would come when the seed would reveal itself on Earth and defeat the enemy that caused the fall in Eden.

In fact, with the manifestation of the Messiah, coming in the flesh, took command of the resumption of the Kingdom that the enemy thought belonged to him and put things in their proper place.

The last Adam, as Jesus was named by Paul, brought the revelation of the Kingdom to man and presented Himself as King.

The first Adam, the one created by God, despite being clothed with glory and honor, with his sin, lost glory and opened the portals of dishonor through which humanity unrestrainedly entered.

Adam and the early members of his family had the overwhelming opportunity to live in the Kingdom one hundred percent. And then they experienced the worst in the world by living the tragedy of dishonor.

Man disconnected from God generates disconnected children Adam's drama was so devastating that it created a dimension that he did not know and that had not yet been revealed.

Let us understand this fact: The Garden of Eden was not just a geographical place. It was a spiritual dimension of government, that is, Eden would be the place where man, Adam would rule the world. In other words, Eden the center of government. And Eden was planned by the Lord in such a way that man, living in the material dimension, could meet the Lord who came from a spiritual dimension.

Eden was the perfect place for both God and man. That's why Adam was crowned with glory and honor.

For You have made him a little lower than the angels,
And You have crowned him with glory and honor.
(Psalm 8:5) NKJV

Sin caused an immeasurable rupture in the relationship between Creator and creature. Separation was inevitable. There was no way God, in His holiness, honor, and glory, would continue to allow man to enjoy His glorious presence. Besides, man had lost the government.

The most traumatic consequence was man leaving a spiritual dimension of government, to live in the dimension of matter, experiencing pain, work, suffering and especially knowing death. Such is the depth of dishonor.

In the dimension of government, God gave him the missions he should carry out within the mentality of kingdom. They weren't religious missions; they were government missions. They all involved glory and honor.

> *Then God blessed them, and God said to them, "Be fruitful and multiply; fill the earth and subdue it; have dominion over the fish of the sea, over the birds of the air, and over every living thing that moves on the earth."*
> *Genesis 1:28*

1. Fruitful

Fruitful multiplication was the main function of the reproductive system of the human being.

The people who would inhabit this kingdom would be the product of the biological multiplication that the Lord established in the couple. The production system of the male seed crossed with the complex and wonderful female fertility system.

The Lord did not need to be creating men and women every day. He delegated this honor to man. The creative power of life. Not even the Angels received this honor.

2. Multiply

This was an honorable mission. God gave Adam the task of multiplying His character in all the citizens of the earth. Take a good look at what God is saying to you, "I want all the inhabitants of this kingdom to be the same as you. Multiply your character, just as you are my image and likeness, pass it on to all the inhabitants of this kingdom."

What the Lord intended is that upon coming to earth to visit the earth, He would find thousands upon thousands of 'Adams' and 'Eves.' All living in purity and holiness, with glory and honor, worshipping the Eternal. It would be the Kingdom of heaven, in deep communion and identity with the Kingdom of the Earth.

3. Fill the Earth

In this order come three aspects that are characteristic of kingdom: supply, satiate and overflow. A kingdom does not live in scarcity. The kingdom provides everything to everyone. Scarcity is a picture of dishonor. Dishonor attracts scarcity. As long as there was a multitude of saints, living in glory and honor, the Eternal would not allow that anything would lack throughout the earth. When Abraham was ninety-nine years old, the Lord appeared to him and said:

> *When Abram was ninety-nine years old, the Lord appeared to Abram and said to him, "I am Almighty God; walk before Me and be blameless.*
> *Genesis 17:1 NKJV*

He is emphasizing that the Kingdom of God is a kingdom of abundance. A kingdom where blessings overflow.

A God of honor is not economical or scarce when it comes to supplying his people. Lack cannot go side by side with abundance.

God the Shadai satisfies all the needs of his Kingdom. Satiates everyone. Its abundance is to give security to the citizens of the Kingdom.

Let's see what happened in the miracle of the multiplication of two fish and five loaves of bread.

When the day began to wear away, the twelve came and said to Him, "Send the multitude away, that they may go into the surrounding towns and country, and lodge and get provisions; for we are in a deserted place here."

> *13 But He said to them, "You give them something to eat." And they said, "We have no more than five loaves and two fish, unless we go and buy food for all these people."*
> *14 For there were about five thousand men. Then He said to His disciples, "Make them sit down in groups of fifty."*
> *15 And they did so, and made them all sit down.*
> *16 Then He took the five loaves and the two fish, and looking up to heaven, He blessed and broke them, and gave them to the disciples to set before the multitude.*
> *17 So they all ate and were filled, and twelve baskets of the leftover fragments were taken up by them.*
> *Luke 9:12-17 NKJV*

3. Subjugate The Earth

The verb subject in this context of Genesis presents a great difficulty of interpretation. A confusion is created with the term dominate. Some even believe that God was repeating the same order. It's not like that. The Lord gave two different orders.

First we will address the order to hold the earth, then elsewhere we will see what it means to dominate.

When the Lord orders man to hold the earth, he is giving him a right that must be exercised with honor.

We find the verb subjugate/subdue in almost the entire Bible. The verb varies its meaning in each context; But its meaning does not vary. That is, holding can have a positive and a negative aspect. The explanation is as follows: Man can hold everything that appeals to him, what is useful and what is necessary. However, you can also hold what is harmful, negative or rejection.

Let's say it in simpler words: One can subject his friends as well as his enemies. When he subjects his friends he does it based on honor. When he subjects his enemies he does so based on authority.

Let's see some examples:

A. The subjection of women

To the woman He said:

"I will greatly multiply your sorrow and your conception;
In pain you shall bring forth children;
Your desire shall be for your husband,
And he shall rule over you."
Genesis 3:16 NKJV

Before sin, the woman was not subjected to the husband. She was a helper and was on the same level. After sin, man receives the power to hold or dominate it. Although she was not an enemy but continued beside the man as a companion and wife but subject to the orders of her husband.

Note, however, that the man was not the "owner" or "lord" of the woman. The man, despite holding her, was to care, protect, love and honor the woman who was now attached to him. And although the woman's desire was for her husband, this did not make her a slave, or her disobedience should result in physical punishment. If the man wished to relate carnally with her for his moments of pleasure, he should do so through a conquest motivated by honor. The man would have to give love if he wanted to receive love from her.

We find the verb subject in the texts that speak of subjecting for love but we also find it in those that speak of subjecting through authority. The latter means submitting the enemy under our will and authority using force and humiliation.

The meaning of the word subject is to make things or people under our subjection serve us according to our interest.

When the Lord commanded that man subdue the earth, he meant to make it a source of blessing to provide food, water and even the natural beauties that bring well-being to man.

Once he held the earth, man had to contribute something to receive the reward. The man had to cultivate, care, plant, conserve, protect the land and do it with a permanent dedication so that she would be a permanent source that meets his needs.

If man honors nature, he would certainly be honored by her. But with regret we see that man degrades nature, cities, rivers and oceans, pollutes the air, explores the soil and seas without a sustainable plan. What do you get back? Deadly diseases, forests turned into deserts, rivers that dry up, millions of human beings and animals starving in so many places on the planet.

Man dishonors the planet God gave him and the planet dishonors the man who lives there. It is the principle of the law that establishes honor for the one who honors, dishonor for the one who dishonors.

This process of divine subjection is the same as that applied to husbands in relation to wives and children. Also, in the employer's relationship with the employees or the shepherd with the sheep.

It applies even in relation to material goods. If one has a rural property and does not give due attention and due care, she will not give her the best of the land.

If a land is poorly maintained or neglected, it happens that the mountain grows, the garbage accumulates, the insects proliferate, the poisonous animals appear, the wells crack, the water breaks down, the animals get sick, the fruits rot. So, the earth will no longer be a blessing for the life of the owner. He held her; But he didn't take care of her.

The subjection from the divine point of view is an attitude of honor.

The shepherds who see the flock, which was given to them by God to care, only as a financial source for their needs and do not care with the honor of the flock of God, are destined to fail.

B.   The Christian's subjection to the Lord

> *Therefore, submit to God. Resist the devil and he will flee from you.*
> *James 4:7 NKJV*

Subjection to the Lord provides you with authority over the devil.

C.   The subjection of the wife to the husband

> *Wives, submit to your own husbands, as to the Lord.*
> *Ephesians 5:22 NKJV*

The subjection to the husband makes her beloved and protected by him.

D.   Subject to the authorities

> *Therefore submit yourselves to every ordinance of man for the Lord's sake, whether to the king as supreme,*
> *1 Peter 2:13 NKJV*

> *Servants, be submissive to your masters with all fear, not only to the good and gentle, but also to the harsh.*
> *1 Peter 2:18 NKJV*

The subjection to the authority provides legal, social security and guarantee of your rights. Who has authority over us provides us with security.

E.   Subject to the pastor

Obey those who rule over you, and be submissive, for they watch out for your souls, as those who must give account. Let them do so with joy and not with grief, for that would be unprofitable for you.
Hebrews 13:17 NKJV

Subjection to the pastor is to obey God and know that there is someone indicated by him to watch over your soul.

We find thousands of texts in the Bible talking about subjection. Here we are not addressing the subjection we make with our enemies or with what is harmful to us. Our dissertation in this book is focused only on the subjection practiced with honor, not the one practiced from the point of view of authority.

In the divine dictionary, to subject means to provide to be provided.

5. Dominate

The command to dominate given to man was very specific from the Lord.

Like the verb "to subject" treated in the previous point, the verb "to dominate" also has two different meanings, one positive and the other negative. It can be used to indicate the positive side in the sense that man has to master what God determined to be dominated. This is the right and positive side.

Mastering what God never sent man ends up being a very serious mistake.

Portuguese-language dictionaries put this word in the sense of exercising authority or power over something or someone.

There is even an application of this word in a neutral sense. We are speaking the Portuguese language.

For example, the soccer player "dominates" the ball. God did not send him to do that, but he also forbade it. In this sense, domination has the sense of ability and not of authority.

When God spoke with marriage about dominance, he used the word "radah." In the Hebrew language it is a plural word, indicating that he spoke to both of them together. In that context, the literal sense is: govern, dominate and exercise absolute control.

The divine order was wisely detailed for the spouses. Adam and Eve had to dominate over the fish in the sea, over the birds of the sky and over all animals that move on the land.

> *Then God blessed them, and God said to them, "Be fruitful and multiply; fill the earth and subdue it; have dominion over the fish of the sea, over the birds of the air, and over every living thing that moves on the earth."*
> *Genesis 1:28 NKJV*

Note that the man was not commanded to exercise dominion over another man. When the man by force of circumstances, professional, social or family, needs to lead or send over another man, the right word is to subject, according to the orientations we glossed in the previous article that deals with the human relationship through subjection.

What we must understand by mastering is to exercise total control over domination. According to the divine order, man should exercise control over the inhabitants of the sea, over the birds that fly through the air and over the animals that inhabit the dry land.

Such living beings should see man as one who is over them and intelligently and wisely manages to dominate over them. That creates fear in dominated animals.

It is interesting to see that dominion when Noah manages to call, order and gather in a unique environment, the Ark, to all the animals that do not live together normally.

They understood Noah's order because he was the dominator. It was the driver wildlife around him.

When the flood ceased and Noah and his family were able to leave the Ark, they received from the Lord the same order that had been given to Adam.

> *So God blessed Noah and his sons, and said to them: "Be fruitful and multiply, and fill the earth.*

2 And the fear of you and the dread of you shall be on every beast of the earth, on every bird of the air, on all that move on the earth, and on all the fish of the sea. They are given into your hand. 3 Every moving thing that lives shall be food for you. I have given you all things, even as the green herbs.
Genesis 9:1-3 NKJV

Fructify, multiply and fill the earth and animals will continue to fear the man who was the dominator.

The domain continued to be the honor of government that man had received in Eden and now continued with Noah and his family.

We will see later in Noah's life that in the likeness of Adam and Eve, dishonor also reached Noah and his family.

Mastering or controlling the land is not a particular authorization to destroy the land. Controlling in this sense was synonymous with preserving, keeping it healthy, productive and beautiful. The Kingdom given to man had to be implanted in a territory that expressed royalty and not misery.

THE FIRST ADAM LOST THAT OPPORTUNITY

The first Adam received everything: Position, government, glory, honor, eternal life, perfect communion with the Creator and a beautiful planet to reign. Sin disconnected him from the Creator and descended from a position of maximum honor to a shameful life of dishonor.

In creation there is a principle: Everything feeds on the source from which it is generated.

If we cut a plant from the earth, we are cutting its connection with the root that is the source that keeps it alive. If we take a fish out of the water, it will die because it was disconnected from its source, which is water. God created us and breathed in us the "ruah" which is the spirit that gives life. With his breath, he gave us life and became our source of life. Sin broke this connection by separating man from his original source.

The man disconnected from his source of honor. He left Eden towards a land where his life would be very hard. He lost all the good that honor gives us.
Created a little less than God and crowned with glory and honor, man with his error descended from his honorable position of government to a dishonorable position of a sinner separated from God.

The powerful and wise divine intervention would be necessary by providing another Adam who did the opposite. An Adam who would take us back from dishonor to the honorable position that, by divine decree and for the love of the eternal Father, belongs to us. God sent another Adam.

CHAPTER 2

JESUS CHRIST: THE SECOND ADAM
FROM DISHONOR TO HONOR

The first prophecy found in the Bible is the Lord himself prophesying to the transgressive couple, announcing that the seed of the woman would bruise/crush the head of the serpent.

And I will put enmity
Between you and the woman,
And between your seed and her Seed;
He shall bruise your head,
And you shall bruise His heel."
Genesis 3:15 NKJV

About four thousand years later, Jesus Christ as the legitimate seed of woman who comes to earth and begins the process of restoring what was lost.

for the Son of Man has come to seek and to save that which was lost.
Luke 9:10 NKJV

The evangelist Luke defines in a peculiar way that Jesus came to seek and save what was lost, not who was lost.

What was lost in sin was the Kingdom and not man. Man was taken to another earthly dimension; but it continued to be the work of the Creation of the Lord. He had no honor but continued to belong to the Lord.

In the previous chapter we mentioned that the first Adam left the position of honor towards a situation of dishonor. Jesus Christ, the last Adam, left his position of honor with the Father to come to earth and do the reverse, that is, to begin in the position of dishonor to bring man to the dimension of honor and place him again in the initial position.

Let this mind be in you which was also in Christ Jesus, 6 who, being in the form of God, did not consider it robbery to be equal with God, 7 but made Himself of no reputation, taking the form of a bondservant, and coming in the likeness of men. 8 And being found in appearance as a man, He humbled Himself and became obedient to the point of death, even the death of the cross. 9 Therefore God also has highly exalted Him and given Him the name which is above every name, 10 that at the name of Jesus every knee should bow, of those in heaven, and of those on earth, and of those under the earth, 11 and that every tongue should confess that Jesus Christ is Lord, to the glory of God the Father.
Philippians 2:5-11 NKJV

This process of self-emptying is known as the doctrine of kenosis , which shows us Christ getting rid of some attributes and prerogatives to live among us.

Notice that in Eden man was created similar to God but when Christ had to come into the world the opposite happened: God became similar to man.

> *but made Himself of no reputation, taking the form of a bondservant, and coming in the likeness of men.*
> *Philippians 2:7 NKJV*

THE OBJECTIVE OF CHRIST WAS TO RESTORE THE KINGDOM

When Christ came to earth his goal was not only to save man from his sins but mainly to resume the rule of the Kingdom that God gave to Adam, the first Adam.

The devil, a liar as always, offered the kingdoms of the world to Jesus. As if they were his, but Jesus rejected him.

> *Then the devil, taking Him up on a high mountain, showed Him all the kingdoms of the world in a moment of time.*

6 And the devil said to Him, "All this authority I will give You, and their glory; for this has been delivered to me, and I give it to whomever I wish. 7 Therefore, if You will worship before me, all will be Yours."

8 And Jesus answered and said to him, "Get behind Me, Satan! For it is written, 'You shall worship the Lord your God, and Him only you shall serve.' "

Luke 4:5-8 NKJV

The devil had deceived Adam and Eve but Jesus did not come to negotiate with the enemy but to take from him what never belonged to him. The Kingdom was given to the first Adam and he lost it with sin. Now the last Adam conquers the devil and retakes his Kingdom. After taking it, Jesus takes man back into his Kingdom.

In this context, it is good to note that when Christ came into the world, he came nothing more as a Savior of men, he came as King. And according to his activities he did not come as a Savior who later became King but came as a King who saved his people. Our understanding is that He is not only a Savior, He is a Savior King of His Kingdom and His people.

Then, Christ came to reconquer the lost Kingdom and give it back to man in the power of his name. Man, in his origin is able to multiply, fill, bear fruit, dominate and subjugate/subdue.

1. He Was Born As King

Although by the force of circumstances Jesus was born in a manger, he came to this world with the aim of restoring the Kingdom and showing who in fact and by law was the King of this Kingdom.

The devil knew that he would come and tried to kill him in various ways so that he never reached the cross. To our happiness, the devil had no knowledge or revelation of the place where he would appear and live. The devil only had the opportunity to meet him when he was already an adult and was baptized in the Jordan River by John the Baptist.

However, there is a very interesting event that occurred in the childhood of Jesus. Although it is not clear the age of the child Jesus, in his early childhood, he was visited by a group of magicians from the east. Even having different opinions, the writers consider that this happened more or less when the child was two years old.

There are also controversies about the number of these magicians and their origins. Some say they were kings; others claim they were astrologers, others even claim they were sorcerers.

Roman Catholic theology provides the number and names, stating that there were three and were called Melchor, Gaspar and Baltazar.

There is also the Jewish tradition that has a version for this visit. Perhaps the Jewish alternative is more valuable to us.

According to this tradition, these magicians were wise, they knew astrology and their ancestors had contact with the prophet Daniel in Babylon where they learned to deal with the stars and prophecy.

When Daniel was established as a teacher of the wise men of Babylon, he ministered and received many offerings for his teachings. Those offerings were gold, silver and some valuable things. They were first fruits that his disciples gave him.

Daniel kept his offerings because he was a captive in Babylon and had no way of spending everything he received.

He prophesied about the coming of the Messiah and had revelation about him. Then he took the riches he had treasured and entrusted them to the disciples who would survive by guiding them to share them from generation to generation until they reached the generation of wise men who had the encounter with Jesus.

Daniel ordered that the offering he entrusted to them should be delivered to the child King that God would send to the Jews. This was done. When the magicians came to Jerusalem, they brought gold, frankincense and myrrh that were offerings of honor to be delivered to the King.

The first offering that Jesus received on earth was an honor offering from one of the wisest Old Testament prophets.

GOLD OFFERING

Gold was the recognition of non-Jewish nations that he would not only be King of the Jews but also of all nations that bowed before him. This means that the kings of the earth submit to the King of the kings.

Remember that those kings were from Persia, Arabia and India, and probably from other nations not cited in tradition.

This offering unleashed the revelation for men that the King who was coming was also a prophet. Fact confirmed at the baptism of Jesus. He was baptized by John the Baptist, another prophet, who publicly confessed that Jesus was greater than him. Jesus, the last Adam, when he came to earth, he did it as King.

INCENSE OFFER

The incense was a kind of milky resin extracted from a tree whose botanical terminology calls it Boswellia Sacra (or Boswellia Carter) and is popularly known as Olíbano, frankincense tree, incense of Olíbano and tree of Lebanon.

The incense was used only by the High Priest and meant the prayer that rose before the Lord.

Now when He had taken the scroll, the four living creatures and the twenty-four elders fell down before the Lamb, each having a harp, and golden bowls full of incense, which are the prayers of the saints.

However, there is a rigorous warning, regarding the incense, established by the Lord to the priests. The incense offered to the Lord could only be used to worship him. And the preparation of incense also obeyed its orientations. It could not be done otherwise. Let's see the composition:

And the Lord said to Moses: "Take sweet spices, stacte and onycha and galbanum, and pure frankincense with these sweet spices; there shall be equal amounts of each.

35 You shall make of these an incense, a compound according to the art of the perfumer, salted, pure, and holy. 36 And you shall beat some of it very fine, and put some of it before the Testimony in the tabernacle of meeting where I will meet with you. It shall be most holy to you. 37 But as for the incense which you shall make, you shall not make any for yourselves, according to its composition. It shall be to you holy for the Lord.
Exodus 30:34-37 NKJV

The Lord determined judgment for whoever made such a composition for himself and not for him. Only the high priest could use it and nothing more than to worship the Lord.
Exodus (30: 34-37)

Whoever makes any like it, to smell it, he shall be cut off from his people." Exodus 30:38 NKJV

When the magicians offered incense to Jesus, they were recognizing him as High Priest. That is, he was King and now he was recognized as High Priest, the only mediator between God and men.

Beyond the honor they were imputing to him, they also recognized him in the prophetic world.

MYRRH OFFERING

Myrrh was the most emblematic present of the three. While gold recognized him as King and incense as High Priest, myrrh was the prophetic act that spoke of his death and resurrection. Myrrh means bitter and was from the regions of North Africa, produced by a thorny tree that could reach up to five meters high. Myrrh, like incense, could serve as a balm to heal wounds and functioned as an anti-inflammatory. It was also used in the production of perfumes.

The most important use was in the embalming practiced in Egypt and other nations of the East. People were embalmed when they died because they believed in his resurrection. Hence the concern of preserving the body for the event of returning to life.

When they offered myrrh as a present to Jesus, they were revealing His prophetic destiny to die for the world and rise again for eternal life.

Imagine someone who has just come to this life and is already receiving information about his death. That is what the magicians did with Jesus. The good part of Jesus' prophetic story is that the offering received also showed faith in the resurrection.

And Nicodemus, who at first came to Jesus by night, also came, bringing a mixture of myrrh and aloes, about a hundred pounds. 40 Then they took the body of Jesus, and bound it in strips of linen with the spices, as the custom of the Jews is to bury.
John 19:39-40 NKJV

2.   During His Ministry He Behaved As King

When his ministry was activated by his mother at the wedding in Cana in Galilee, his "carpenter's son" behavior changed and he began to show a way of acting that surprised everyone. He was now under divine guidance to fulfill what was commanded and began to use King's language and King's behavior as we will see below in some New Testament passages.
At the wedding in Cana in Galilee.

The first two chapters of the Gospel of John give us an admirable vision of Jesus' behavior change as the day of his activation as the Messiah, and his position as King, arrived.

a)   John the Baptist revealed his real, priestly and prophetic identity

This is He of whom I said, 'After me comes a Man who is preferred before me, for He was before me.'

31 I did not know Him; but that He should be revealed to Israel, therefore I came baptizing with water."

32 And John bore witness, saying, "I saw the Spirit descending from heaven like a dove, and He remained upon Him.

33 I did not know Him, but He who sent me to baptize with water said to me, 'Upon whom you see the Spirit descending, and remaining on Him, this is He who baptizes with the Holy Spirit.'

34 And I have seen and testified that this is the Son of God."

John 1:30-34 NKJV

b) The revelation of John the Baptist alone generated disciples of the Messiah

Again, the next day, John stood with two of his disciples. 36 And looking at Jesus as He walked, he said, "Behold the Lamb of God!"

37 The two disciples heard him speak, and they followed Jesus. 38 Then Jesus turned, and seeing them following, said to them, "What do you seek?"

They said to Him, "Rabbi" (which is to say, when translated, Teacher), "where are You staying?"

39 He said to them, "Come and see." They came and saw where He was staying, and remained with Him that day (now it was about the tenth hour).

40 One of the two who heard John speak, and followed Him, was Andrew, Simon Peter's brother. 41 He first found his own brother Simon, and said to him, "We have found the Messiah" (which is translated, the Christ).
John 1:35-41 NKJV

The anointing of the Messiah, activated by the revelation of John the Baptist, begins to attract future apostles to the King. Honor attracts followers to join the King.

The anointing walks along with honor. Honor never departs from the anointing.

c) The King, without asking their opinion, began to determine changes in the disciples' lives even before discipling them.
And he brought him to Jesus.

Now when Jesus looked at him, He said, "You are Simon the son of Jonah. You shall be called Cephas" (which is translated, A Stone).
John 1:42 NKJV

He changed Peter's name and he didn't ask why.
Imagine Peter coming home, and his wife asks: "Where were you Simon?" And he answers: "Woman, as of today I am no longer called Simon, my name is now Peter."

She asks again: "What is the idea of changing your name?" And Peter informs her: "It was not me but Jesus. He looked at me, identified me and immediately changed my name. I was ashamed to question him because after all he is the King. From what I understand, my life from now on will change."

The following day Jesus wanted to go to Galilee, and He found Philip and said to him, "Follow Me."
John 1:43 NKJV

He ordered Philip to follow him. Felipe did not ask: Why should I follow you? No one questions the King. The King is obeyed.
Now Philip was from Bethsaida, the city of Andrew and Peter. 45 Philip found Nathanael and said to him, "We have found Him of whom Moses in the law, and also the prophets, wrote—Jesus of Nazareth, the son of Joseph."
46 And Nathanael said to him, "Can anything good come out of Nazareth?"
Philip said to him, "Come and see."
47 Jesus saw Nathanael coming toward Him, and said of him, "Behold, an Israelite indeed, in whom is no deceit!"
48 Nathanael said to Him, "How do You know me?"
Jesus answered and said to him, "Before Philip called you, when you were under the fig tree, I saw you."
John 1:44-48 NKJV

He won Nathanael with a blunt and admirable revelation that was only known to him and his mother.

In Israel there is a certain mysticism about some plants such as the fig tree, the olive tree, the vine, the date, etc.

According to rabbinic tradition, the fig tree would be the tree of knowledge under which the Jews used to sit down to take advantage of their shadow and meditate on the law and the prophets.

With this data, Jesus knowing about Nathanael's intelligence gave him the following message: "I know where you were and where you came from, now you will walk and live with me and I will take you to eternity. Under the fig tree you were protected from physical death but could not escape spiritual death; but walking with me you will be protected from the power of death. By my death, I will give you eternal life."

The disciples perceived that they were really before the King, who knew the past, the present and the future and who determines the facts according to his will. See how Nathanael recognizes him as King:

Nathanael answered and said to Him, "Rabbi, You are the Son of God! You are the King of Israel!"
John 1:49 NKJV

d) He confronted his mother in Cana in Galilee.

On the third day there was a wedding in Cana of Galilee, and the mother of Jesus was there. 2 Now both Jesus and His disciples were invited to the wedding. 3 And when they ran out of wine, the mother of Jesus said to Him, "They have no wine."
4 Jesus said to her, "Woman, what does your concern have to do with Me? My hour has not yet come."
John 2:1-4 NKJV

Mary spoke with Jesus in a blunt and clear way that the wine was over. It was the end of the old wine and the beginning of the new wine. It was the beginning of Christ's ministry.

Jesus' response indicates that he understood what Mary was revealing to him and confronted her not as a beloved son but as the King who was now on his mission, knowing that from now on Mary, his beloved mother, could no longer tell him what "What should I do?" In other words, he meant: "I know that I am the new wine, but the time has not yet come to introduce myself doing miracles everywhere. Miracles are now for the glory and honor of the one Who sent me. I am here to do His will and that of no one else."

Mary understood that from that moment on, Jesus was no longer her son, but now he was the Christ, the Messiah. The Savior who would save her from her sins. The King who would rule and protect her.

Mary finished her mission and Christ began his.

e) He physically confronted the street vendors who traded in the courtyard of the Temple.

Now the Passover of the Jews was at hand, and Jesus went up to Jerusalem. 14 And He found in the temple those who sold oxen and sheep and doves, and the money changers doing business. 15 When He had made a whip of cords, He drove them all out of the temple, with the sheep and the oxen, and poured out the changers' money and overturned the tables. 16 And He said to those who sold doves, "Take these things away! Do not make My Father's house a house of merchandise!"
John 2:13-16 NKJV

Who has the courage to face an angry King? Brave, strong and determined as it suits a King. He faced everyone without even asking his disciples for help. King is king.

f) The Jews tried to confront him and he faced them, and being angry, he was even more blunt.

So the Jews answered and said to Him, "What sign do You show to us, since You do these things?"
19 Jesus answered and said to them, "Destroy this temple, and in three days I will raise it up."
20 Then the Jews said, "It has taken forty-six years to build this temple, and will You raise it up in three days?"
21 But He was speaking of the temple of His body.
John 2:18-21 NKJV

Jesus was revealing himself as greater than the Temple they idolized. He was saying: This is the Temple, but I am the King.

g) He decided to stay at the house of Zacchaeus although he was not invited.

Then Jesus entered and passed through Jericho. 2 Now behold, there was a man named Zacchaeus who was a chief tax collector, and he was rich.
3 And he sought to see who Jesus was, but could not because of the crowd, for he was of short stature.
4 So he ran ahead and climbed up into a sycamore tree to see Him, for He was going to pass that way.

5 And when Jesus came to the place, He looked up and saw him, and said to him, "Zacchaeus, make haste and come down, for today I must stay at your house."
Luke 19:1-5 NKJV

A King does not need an invitation. He decides where he wants to pose and nobody would contradict him.

Imagine Zacchaeus arriving home agitated and saying to his wife: "Darling prepare things quickly because Jesus is coming to stay here today"
The woman replies: "How so? So suddenly? Without warning? Who invited him?"
Zacchaeus continues: "No one invited him. He looked at me and said he would stay at my house today. Then he sent me down quickly from the sycamore he was in. And even more, he comes with 12 disciples."
Zacchaeus' house was not his, it was King Jesus.
Jesus behaved as King where he passed. Authority of King, position of King and spoke like King.

h) He ordered to bring a donkey from a Jewish citizen.

When He had said this, He went on ahead, going up to Jerusalem.

*29 And it came to pass, when He drew near to Bethphage and Bethany, at the mountain called Olivet, that He sent two of His disciples, 30 saying, "Go into the village opposite you, where as you enter you will find a colt tied, on which no one has ever sat. Loose it and bring it here. 31 And if anyone asks you, 'Why are you loosing it?' thus you shall say to him, 'Because the Lord has need of it.' "
32 So those who were sent went their way and found it just as He had said to them. 33 But as they were loosing the colt, the owners of it said to them, "Why are you loosing the colt?" 34 And they said, "The Lord has need of him." 35 Then they brought him to Jesus. And they threw their own clothes on the colt, and they set Jesus on him. 36 And as He went, many spread their clothes on the road.*
Luke 19:28-36 NKJV

Like the house of Zacchaeus, the colt was not of the Jewish citizen, it was of King Jesus.

i) He entered Jerusalem presenting himself as King, ignoring any Jewish or Roman authority.

And as He went, many spread their clothes on the road. 37 Then, as He was now drawing near the descent of the Mount of Olives,

the whole multitude of the disciples began to rejoice and praise God with a loud voice for all the mighty works they had seen,
38 saying:
" 'Blessed is the King who comes in the name of the Lord!' Peace in heaven and glory in the highest!"
John 19:36-38 NKJV

Jesus entered as King in his city being loved, adored and acclaimed by the people. That was a moment of joy and happiness in his ministry.

Zacchaeus' house, the Jew's colt and the city of Jerusalem always belonged to Him. It was the men who never realized that. Also, today, your car, your home, your job, your money, your family, your health and even you belong to Him.

He is the king. He is sovereign. He commands. He reigns and from him the honor flows in our favor.

And we say: To Him all the glory, honor and praise.

If you continue reading the Bible, you will find many other passages where you will see the behavior of Jesus as King. Be in the requirement of the place for the last dinner.

Be in the confrontation with the rabbis and even with the Roman authorities, mainly with Pontius Pilate.

In front of Pilate, Jesus declared himself King and identified his Kingdom.
They will scourge Him and kill Him. And the third day He will rise again."
34 But they understood none of these things; this saying was hidden from them, and they did not know the things which were spoken.
35 Then it happened, as He was coming near Jericho, that a certain blind man sat by the road begging. 36 And hearing a multitude passing by, he asked what it meant. 37 So they told him that Jesus of Nazareth was passing by.
John 18:33-37 NKJV

He was born as King and lived as King.

3. He Died As King

At the death of Jesus, Pontius Pilate, motivated by circumstances, sent a sentence to be written at the top of the cross: "Jesus Nazarene King of the Jews."
Without knowing it, he wrote a prophetic title, and he did it in three languages, Hebrew, Greek and Latin.

That Nazarene Jew was not only the King of the Jews but the King of the whole earth. The King of all nations. The eternal King

The religious leaders tried to eliminate the title but Pilate stood firm and did not let anyone modify anything: "What I have written, I have written"
John 19:22.

Once dead he received a funeral worthy of a King. The mortuary protocol was: Clean sheets and a grave that had never been used.

Jesus was born of a virgin, entered Jerusalem mounted on a virgin colt that had never been ridden and was placed in a virgin sepulcher that had never been used. All these things were first fruits for the King who came to earth in substitution of the first Adam.

Jesus was born as King, lived as King and died as King.

4. He Rose As King

When Jesus rose he did so with a different appearance. Perhaps that made it difficult for them to recognize the women who went to the grave and confused him with the gardener.

He had no wounds or blood or any sign that the resurrected man was the same one who had been buried three days before. New appearance and new clothes. Those garments are one of the mysteries of the Bible. With that garment Jesus went up to heaven. If that garment could leave the earth and enter the celestial dimension, they could only have come from there.

To resurrect Him as King, He received the adoration of women:

And as they went to tell His disciples, behold, Jesus met them, saying, "Rejoice!" So they came and held Him by the feet and worshiped Him.
Matthew 28:9 NKJV

In the resurrection he revives with full powers:
And Jesus came and spoke to them, saying, "All authority has been given to Me in heaven and on earth.
Matthew 28:18 NKJV

Upon returning to the heavenly home, King Jesus returned invested with all power and authority that manifested the character of a King and his Kingdom.

He was born as King, lived as King, died as King and rose as King.

5. He Entered Heaven As King

He was received in heaven as King. The angels have no omniscience than an exclusive attribute of the Lord, so they had expectation of His return. The angels wanted to know how His life was on earth. For this reason, seeing Him, He was worshiped and sang to. See Psalm 24.

> *Lift up your heads, O you gates!*
> *And be lifted up, you everlasting doors!*
> *And the King of glory shall come in.*
> *Who is this King of glory?*
> *The Lord strong and mighty,*
> *The Lord mighty in battle.*
> *Lift up your heads, O you gates!*
> *Lift up, you everlasting doors!*
> *And the King of glory shall come in.*
> *Who is this King of glory?*
> *The Lord of hosts,*
> *He is the King of glory. Selah*
> *Psalm 24: 7-10 NKJV*

Jesus was born as King, lived as King, died as King, rose as King and was received in heaven as King.

6. When he returns to earth, he will return as King. The Bible declares Jesus' promised that He would return to earth. We believe in that. But under what conditions will He return?

The apostle John reveals to us in Revelation:

11 Now I saw heaven opened, and behold, a white horse. And He who sat on him was called Faithful and True, and in righteousness He judges and makes war. 12 His eyes were like a flame of fire, and on His head were many crowns. He had a name written that no one knew except Himself. 13 He was clothed with a robe dipped in blood, and His name is called The Word of God. 14 And the armies in heaven, clothed in fine linen, white and clean, followed Him on white horses. 15 Now out of His mouth goes a [c]sharp sword, that with it He should strike the nations. And He Himself will rule them with a rod of iron. He Himself treads the winepress of the fierceness and wrath of Almighty God. 16 And He has on His robe and on His thigh a name written:
Revelation 19:11-16 NKJV

When Jesus entered Jerusalem riding a colt, he entered as a King of peace. Now he is riding a white horse. Kings used to use horses when they went to battles. He now does not come as King of peace, he comes as a King who comes to subdue all the kingdoms of the world and ultimately establish His Kingdom on earth, defeating all the enemies who for centuries dared to challenge him and tried to destroy his Kingdom on earth.

His clothes are stained with blood, his eyes are like a flame of fire. His Word will function as a powerful sword destroying all thought and all haughty or deceptive argument that has been formed in people's minds for centuries.

He comes to win. Maranata!

He was born as King, lived as King, died as King, rose as King, was received in heaven as King and will return to earth as King of kings and Lord of lords.

COMPARISON OF CHAPTERS 1 AND 2

It is my hope that by comparing the two chapters we have just broken down; the reader can easily distinguish the difference between the first and the last Adam.

While the first was crowned with glory and honor to be created and installed on earth to rule it; the second came in dishonor and conquered the lost honor and restored the multitude that was lost because of the sin of the first Adam.

For the honor to return, contrary to the situation of Eden where man received it as a gift, now man needs to conquer it. Man needs to learn to live in honor. Only in that way will your life be worthy of worshiping and living in the presence of God.

Christians today persist in a simply religious vision in relationships with the Lord. This religious vision is wrong. Religion lives on dogmas and rules. The Kingdom of God is based on eternal foundations and principles of life for our horizontal relationships with our fellow men and our vertical relationships with the Lord.

As a spiritual being, man has the power on earth to operate as God, to be as God. That is what God wants from each of us. But; how do we operate in this way if we have not learned the law of the Lord? How do we serve a King of whom we do not know his will? How do we receive honor if we do not honor the Lord or our brothers?

A man can have access in the condition of dishonor (guided only by instincts, by his knowledge) to a scenario where only real functions can be understood by the Spirit. God wants to return man to the condition he had in Eden, where he had intimacy and direct relationship, and where there was no fear, being in glory and honor.

Then, the purpose of Jesus, the last Adam, was to recover the image and likeness and honor of man's government. When God restores things, he does it in the best way. He always increases, he adds.

Kingdom is dominion, so the Church needs the Kingdom of God to be applied and lived so that it can manifest and materialize.

Jesus came with that purpose. That was his message, that was his ministry. He had a Kingdom mission, so he said that being born again had to do with the ability to see and enter the life of the Kingdom.

Then, man receives the connection of life again. Jesus breathed on the disciples after he was resurrected and said that he is a life-giving Spirit as Adam was a living soul.

For the man to be able to resume his environment and his government, God did not have a religious service problem; but of government. God does not need religious services or songs, He needs worshipers. That is what He told the Samaritan woman.

He who knows how to reign knows how to worship.

We always want to do services and songs that refer to our pain. Our worship is almost always related to our needs and requests to God.

> *I will sing with the spirit but I will also sing with the understanding. We must think well to sing well. We must have a Kingdom mentality like David. While the Church cultivates the mentality of priest, of Church worship, it will be like sheep.*
>
> *But when he begins to think like a king, he will look like a son, as heirs.*
>
> *Now I say that the heir, as long as he is a child, does not differ at all from a slave, though he is master of all, 2 but is under guardians and stewards until the time appointed by the father. 3 Even so we, when we were children, were in bondage under the elements of the world. 4 But when the fullness of the time had come, God sent forth His Son, born of a woman, born under the law, 5 to redeem those who were under the law, that we might receive the adoption as sons. 6 And because you are sons, God has sent forth the Spirit of His Son into your hearts, crying out, "Abba, Father!" 7 Therefore you are no longer a slave but a son, and if a son, then an heir of God through Christ.*
>
> *Galatians 4:1-7 NKJV*

Honor is one of the eternal foundations. It comes from the creation of the eternal Kingdom of our God.

Let us live in honor and we will be honored. If we live in dishonor, we will be dishonored.

The choice will always be ours.

CHAPTER 3

THERE IS NO KINGDOM WITHOUT HONOR

17 Honor all people. Love the brotherhood. Fear God. Honor the king.
1 Peter 2:17 NKJV

Honor should never be relegated to the background in the lives of those who follow Christ. The followers of the Messiah walk in honor. If they do not, their spiritual life does not have the quality they should have and their testimony is negatively compromised. It becomes a testimony worthless, without honor.

Honor is one of the foundations of the Kingdom of God in the Bible. There is no one who can relate to the Eternal except through the path of honor.

When one goes to the presence of the King, summoned or invited, the first contact is always the moment of honor.

16 "Three times a year all your males shall appear before the Lord your God in the place which He chooses: at the Feast of Unleavened Bread, at the Feast of Weeks, and at the Feast of Tabernacles; and they shall not appear before the Lord empty-handed.
Deuteronomy 16:16 NKJV

19 "All that open the womb are Mine, and every male firstborn among your livestock, whether ox or sheep. 20 But the firstborn of a donkey you shall redeem with a lamb. And if you will not redeem him, then you shall break his neck. All the firstborn of your sons you shall redeem.
"And none shall appear before Me empty-handed.
Exodus 34:19-20 NKJV

2. HONOR: THE SENSE OF THE WORSHIP OF GOD

When presenting yourself before the Lord of your life, do not do so only to make material requests but with the intention of worshiping him. Do it even if you are going to ask for something later. And remember that there is no worship without offering. There is no worship with empty hands or empty heart. Honor is a delivery.

Honor is the conjunction of all virtues, it is good moral behavior in the Christian walk and fulfill the ethically correct, both with others and with oneself.

Our example is the Lord Jesus Christ. When he visited the earth in human form and taught us with word and with examples the true meaning of honor. No one on earth can claim ignorance about honor if Christ's example is public and notorious, and his example is an inheritance for all who wish to live in honor.

Several times Jesus referred to the Father in an attitude of honor. He was never noticed any gesture of disobedience. No word or phrase of murmuring ever came out of his mouth. At no time did he complain about his fate or the struggles and lacks he had on earth. Not even when he was savagely beaten by his enemies who set him on and tortured him.

The Bible affirms that Jesus was obedient until death, and death of the cross. Jesus is the perfect example of how we should live and teach our children how to proceed.

8 And being found in appearance as a man, He humbled Himself and became obedient to the point of death, even the death of the cross.
Philippians 2:8 NKJV

By observing the words, attitudes and wisdom of Jesus we are all admired. He knew how to treat people with a simple word. Even in the face of injustices, he taught not to pay badly for evil but with good and forgiveness. He was the man of the second, third and thousands of opportunities to start over. Until today none of his words fell to the ground. He himself said:

35 Heaven and earth will pass away, but My words will by no means pass away.
Matthew 24:35 NKJV

The words out of the mouth of a man of honor are precious and powerful words. These words have a great weight in the spiritual life.

3. HONOR AND DISHONOR PERSIST IN MAN

Every man born on earth brings within him the seed of honor and the seed of dishonor. Man is programmed by God to live in honor during his life; but when he decides to change the divine design for human programming based on the sinful system, he begins to enjoy the disgrace of a dishonored life.

Everyone can live with honor by being weak or strong, having money or not, being educated or uneducated. The social position is not a solid argument to justify a dishonored life.

God prefers to work with men of honor because he is a God of honor. Being that honor one of the fundamentals, everyone needs to establish themselves on that basis. When God seeks someone in the world, he initiates the process of total change so that the dishonored found will be transformed and established in a position of honor, so that he can fulfill his prophetic destiny.

One of the emblematic events of the beginning of humanity is the case between Cain and Abel, which we will explain in one of the chapters later in this book.

There we will notice the fight between honor and dishonor that began with those two young people and endures to this day, and will surely last until Christ returns to establish his Kingdom in this world.

It is clear that beyond religion there are many people who choose to live an honest life, and sometimes they are chosen by God precisely because they already live in a state of honor and present the ideal conditions to fulfill God's purpose in their projects.

4. THE EXAMPLE OF JOSÉ

A notable example is the case of a marriage prepared by God to receive the Messiah in his house who would change the history of mankind. It was an honest marriage.

Joseph and Mary represent at the beginning of the New Testament an example of people whose character is the clear proof of their ethical strength.

Let's see some virtues that are a great indication that Joseph was a man of honor in the society in which he lived.

a)	Moral Integrity

Jewish and Christian traditions show Joseph as a great example of integrity in his time. There are no records or notes in his biography that describe him as a useless or irresponsible man.

A man who enjoys moral integrity has self-control and lives a integral life.

> *18 Now the birth of Jesus Christ was as follows: After His mother Mary was betrothed to Joseph, before they came together, she was found with child of the Holy Spirit. 19 Then Joseph her husband, being a just man, and not wanting to make her a public example, was minded to put her away secretly.*
> *Matthew 1:18-19 NKJV*

Being a man of integrity would never defame the one with whom he was already committed to marry.

A popular saying goes like this: "Who is ashame is not ashamed."

Rabbinic thinking states: "Your honor is more valuable than your money."

b)   Excellent Reputation

Joseph was a cabinetmaker, a trade specialized at that time that produced great profits. This placed him in a stable and well-being condition. Something like an upper middleclass person today.

Joseph was a professional so famous that people called him the carpenter. It was easy to find him because of the reputation he enjoyed due to the art of his trade.

When Joseph died, Jesus must have been about 14 or 15 years old. From then on, Jesus had to take up his father's job to support his family. Being the firstborn, he had such responsibility.

Upon assuming his ministry and beginning to preach, an interesting fact occurred: In his comings and goings, he came to Nazareth one day and went to minister in the synagogue. His preaching impressed the listeners so that they were amazed; but some critics also appeared. See how they identified it:

54 When He had come to His own country, He taught them in their synagogue, so that they were astonished and said, "Where did this Man get this wisdom and these mighty works?

55 Is this not the carpenter's son? Is not His mother called Mary? And His brothers James, Joses, Simon, and Judas?
Matthew 13:54-55 NKJV

Although Joseph had died at least 15 years before, his reputation remained untouched. A man dies; but honor survives him. That is why Jesus was called: "the carpenter's son."

Joseph Was A Man With Honor.

c) Work Dedication

In the same verse that identifies Jesus as "the carpenter's son" it can be noted that Joseph's office gave him an ex officio identity. Only those who work with dedication and love can be identified by their trade. A bad professional will never be identified like this. On the contrary if a professional does not work with bold effort and love for what he does, he will receive pejorative nicknames.

Dedication Is Characteristic Of Someone Who Has Honor.

d)   Protective Father

Before Jesus arrived home, Joseph probably would not have understood the dimension of the cause that God was giving into his hands.

But the facts and phenomena that occurred during the birth of Jesus made him understand the revelation that the angel had revealed to him in dreams.

Therefore, Joseph knew that he must be a father who was deployed effectively, vigilantly and protectively with that child. From the arrival of the child, he would have to develop all the virtues of fatherhood that God gave man to his children.

Paternity in the broadest sense can only be exercised by those who know that being a father is no accident. It is a family ministry. A ministry whose exercise can only and should be carried out in the dimension of honor. Parents honor their children. Children honor their parents. Joseph's effort was so great that he often had to leave his job in the background to take care of the son who was not his; But I was under his responsibility.

So, he left the cabinetmaker's workshop to flee to Egypt when Herod wanted to kill the boy.

13 Now when they had departed, behold, an angel of the Lord appeared to Joseph in a dream, saying, "Arise, take the young Child and His mother, flee to Egypt, and stay there until I bring you word; for Herod will seek the young Child to destroy Him."
Matthew 2:13 NKJV

Joseph dedicated himself to the boy. He honored God faithfully fulfilling his task.

e)   Total Loyalty

Maria's pregnancy was not in Joseph's plans, especially because she had no relationship with him. However, when the angel spoke to him, he accepted the situation and never opened his mouth to make any comments of disappointment about Mary's behavior.

For him it was a great test; but men of honor always succeed in great trials.

In this incident, Joseph was faithful to God, faithful to his wife and faithful to his own dignity.

The man of honor always ends up strengthened when God makes him go through great trials.

f)   Nobility in Critical Moments

Do you know what an attitude of nobility is? Have you ever seen a man of dishonor have noble attitudes?

An incident occurred with Jesus when He was in Jerusalem for Easter and to perform His bar-mitzvah.

When He separated from his family, He was found three days later sitting in the Temple arguing with the rabbis doctors of the law.

When His parents arrived at the premises, Joseph had to question Jesus for his absence, that was a task of rebuke from the father; but it was Mary who caught his attention about being in the Temple before the rabbis and Mary did not even wait for Joseph to reprimand the boy.

At that time, the nobility of Joseph was remarkable, who did not bother himself because his wife took the lead in that rebuke, nor did he feel humiliated or disrespected because he knew that the boy had a special bond with his mother.

Although perhaps he did not fully understand that link, but he knew that the child demanded special attention from her and she participated in raising him in a way that did not apply to her other children.

Joseph understood that and was gentle with his wife. He had an attitude of honor.

g)   Generosity and a Good Dose of Altruism

Although generosity can be confused with the nobility, she goes a little further because she demands gestures of attitude to show herself.

Upon learning of the pregnancy of his promised wife, Joseph's first thought was that he had been betrayed. A man betrayed in the marriage relationship knows that the first thing that is destroyed in their relationship is honor.

When a man goes through an extreme situation like this, if he does not live in honor but in dishonor, the initial step is to humiliate the person who committed the betrayal. Sometimes, the dishonor of one is washed with the dishonor of the other person.

The person of honor, who has nobility, needs to show generosity to overcome such aggression to his honor. Joseph was generous to plan to leave the relationship without pointing out or implying any negative information about his young fiancée.

> 19 Then Joseph her husband, being a just man, and not wanting to make her a public example, was minded to put her away secretly.
> Matthew 1:19 NKJV

See what a wonder: Noble, fair, generous. Who would not want to have such a character?

Joseph knew that with his attitude he protected the physical integrity of his fiancée and the baby in his womb.

He was not selfish thinking about his reputation. He had a forgiving heart that is typical of men and women of honor. Men who forgive and pay evil with good are true giants of faith in the Kingdom of God.

His generosity was not there but was also applied in the upbringing of the child. He agreed to partially renounce his office and the workshop to help his blessed wife take care of the child who would be the Savior of the world, including her own Savior.

h)   Obedient

Unlike other biblical characters, such as Sara who laughed when she heard that her husband would be a father; or Zacharias, the old priest, who doubted when the angel told him that he would be a father; Joseph heard the message and, knowing who was speaking, did not hesitate at any time.

Joseph understood that those words came directly from the Lord and accepted to be a fearful and obedient servant to God. He assumed all the emotional and spiritual burden for having been chosen for a task that most men, if they had known, would have offered to take their place.

Joseph's ministry was the ministry of fatherhood. He did not need to evangelize the entire region of Nazareth or go out preaching the good news. He should only be the faithful father who took care of the Son of God and the other biological children, fruit of his love with the sweet Mary.

His obedience demonstrated how a fearful and honest servant who lives the purpose established by God can make a difference in society. Joseph performed his task with such efficiency that he provided Jesus with the special atmosphere in the family so that he would grow and live the best of his life. See what Lucas narrates:

> 52 And Jesus increased in wisdom and stature, and in favor with God and men.
> Luke 2:52 NKJV

Jesus was formed in a family of honor. No one can deny Joseph's merits in what God entrusted to him. God trusts men of honor.

i)   Honorability

I could use the same word that Matthew used saying that Joseph was a righteous; but I preferred to call him honorable because everything just wins the respect of his peers and they treat him with honorability and reverence.

> 19 Then Joseph her husband, being a just man, and not wanting to make her a public example, was minded to put her away secretly.
> Matthew 1:19 NKJV

In the Bible, the term "just" has a peculiar meaning because the just is always related to the fulfillment, respect and obedience of the Greater Law which is the Torah. However, beyond religious practice, the just is a man who fulfills his civil, legal and family obligations.

In other words, it is not enough to be a religious and not honor their commitments to the government and to the people with whom they have business relationships. He is a man who honors his family responsibilities.

Joseph's behavior towards society credited him as a fair man. It was not he himself who described himself as just but the community in which he lived applied such an adjective. To the point that Matthew in writing his gospel recalled this feature of his character.

He was a fair man. He was an honorable man. He was a man of honor.

5. HONOR: ONE OF THE KINGDOM'S FOUNDATIONS

In the Bible, from Genesis to Revelation, we find many accounts of manifestation of honor. It should not surprise us because throughout the Bible the Kingdom of God is presented to man in various situations. Each time the Kingdom is mentioned, its form and its characteristics are displayed in such a way that its eternity is indisputable. The Kingdom of God is eternal. In the biblical concept, everything that is eternal has no beginning or end. The Kingdom is supported by its foundations that are also eternal.

The Kingdom of God is not static, it is dynamic. When moving, its foundations give it stability so that it remains in spite of adverse circumstances. Such stability is manifested by the children of God who are citizens of this Kingdom.

This manifestation does not occur in dishonored children but in children of honor. Do not worry if one day you lived in dishonor and was rescued by Christ. When he rescued you, according to soteriology, he transported you from the darkness to the Kingdom of the Son of his love.

13 He has delivered us from the power of darkness and conveyed us into the kingdom of the Son of His love, Colossians 1:13 NKJV

When you were introduced to the Kingdom of his Son, you became a citizen of honor. Your attitudes and behavior are now manifestations of honor that glorify and exalt the name of the Lord.

CHAPTER 4

THE PRINCIPLE OF HONOR IN THE KINGDOM OF GOD

We have ministered in our seminars in the Churches on authority, justice and other determining virtues for the proper functioning of the Kingdom of God. All these virtues are originated in the Lord and must manifest themselves in the children of the Kingdom. Something strange happens with the Christian who does not manifest such virtues daily in his relationship with the Lord and with his fellow men. You should review your behavior and correct it immediately if you want to continue enjoying the heavenly blessings.

Honor is part of that set of virtues, commandments and laws that are the fundamental columns established by the Eternal to establish his Kingdom among men.

Honor is one of the prominent foundations of the Kingdom of God for its visibility, that is, because it is noted by those inside and outside the Kingdom of God.

Those inside are admired and exalted and those outside claim that honesty must be part of the Christian's character.
Even Jesus was demanded and criticized by the enemies of the Kingdom for their courageous, honest and loving posture towards those in need.

Some said he acted under the authority of demons without respecting his honor and his person.

> *15 But some of them said, "He casts out demons by [a]Beelzebub, the ruler of the demons."*
> *Luke 11:15 NKJV*

> *24 Now when the Pharisees heard it they said, "This fellow does not cast out demons except by Beelzebub, the ruler of the demons."*
> *Matthew 12:24 NKJV*

> *22 And the scribes who came down from Jerusalem said, "He has Beelzebub," and, "By the ruler of the demons He casts out demons."*
> *Mark 3:22 NKJV*

Note that they are different groups with the same accusation. First the townspeople, then the Pharisees, and finally, the Scribes.

Enemies who live in dishonor join together to fight the citizens of honor. That comes from the beginning of humanity when one brother killed the other because he felt hurt because his brother received honor and he was dishonored by his bad heart.

In the foundations of the Kingdom, honor comes shortly after the foundation of unity.

MEANING OF THE WORD HONOR
What does the word honor mean?

If we take the dictionaries of the Portuguese language as a base, we will find a series of meanings linked to a huge variety of human actions that point to their use in sustaining relations between men, shaping the character of society.

We will see in the definitions taken from the Portuguese language dictionaries that the human being lives situations of honor from his birth to his death. Honor survives the death of the man of honor.

Honor never dies. Honor lives forever.
https://www.dicio.com.br/
Meaning of honor:
Female noun
Principle of conduct of who is virtuous, brave, honest and whose qualities are considered virtuous.
The feeling of that person: ie... He kept the honor as president.
Featured position: director of honor.
Action of worshiping or worshiping a divinity or saint; Worship: celebration in honor of God.

Characteristic of one that is pure or chaste; chastity.
Behavior that denotes consideration: the honor of a dance.
Plural feminine noun
Respect for people who deserve to stand out; Tribute: The teacher is worthy of all honors.

Expression
Lady of honor. Designation of the creature, usually a girl, who carries the rings at the marriage ceremony; little lady.

AURÉLIO DICTIONARY

1. Honor
2. Confer honor to.
3. Distinguish.
4. Ennoble.
5. Venerate
6. To illustrate.
7. Pay the withdrawal made by (a signature).
8. Feeling flattered
9. Reputation as honor.
10. Appreciate

MICHAELIS DICTIONARY
Honor

Female noun

Moral and ethical principle that guides someone to seek to deserve and maintain the consideration of others in society.
Consideration or homage to virtue, to the good moral, artistic, professional qualities of a person.

Consideration and tribute paid to a person, a holiness or an important event: "... that day a bottle of Porto wine was opened and the two drank in honor of the great event.
Feeling of glory and greatness; splendor.

Feeling and attitude of consideration, deference and proof of appreciation.
Important position or function achieved by someone in a hierarchy: "Fernanda had formed a company ... and placed JK, then exiled in Portugal, as honorary president of the company"
Female sexual purity; chastity; virginity.
Honor
Plural feminine noun
Honors given in homage to someone for conduct or exemplary deed: "They were ... received in their land with hero honors"
Honorary title of a position.

With this information in tow we have for sure all possible definitions about the word honor. If you consult other dictionaries you will find the same meaning explained here although perhaps with other terms.

In the Kingdom of God, because it is a foundation of the Kingdom, honor is directly and widely connected to all those who claim to have given their lives to Jesus and follow him.

It is likely that you know of many who call themselves Christians living their lives totally away from honor. However, observe how your personal, professional, spiritual and emotional life is. In this case the logic is perverse: Who does not live in honor, because he lives in dishonor. Honor has its blessings guaranteed. Dishonor also has its punishments programmed and executed.

THE WORD HONOR IN THE BIBLE

The word honor is of Hebrew origin and can be a verb as well as a noun, depending on its place in the sentence.

Throughout this study we will have several words that have the meaning of honor. The meaning varies according to the goal of honor that may be God, family, parents, kings, authorities, prophets, ministers, people, objects, cities, nations, etc. The important thing is to notice that honor appears everywhere and leads us to assume it as a lifestyle. It is not worth living without honor.

Among the cases of honor mentioned in the Old Testament, perhaps the best known is God's command to honor parents.

12 "Honor your father and your mother, that your days may be long upon the land which the Lord your God is giving you.
Exodus 20:12 NKJV

In this verse the original word is "kabed"

CONFUSION WITH THE TERM GLORIFY

Some confusion usually occurs between honoring and glorifying that "kabod" is written in Hebrew. Many preachers and teachers apply the word honor where it should be to glorify and vice versa. In the case to see next, the glory went away because the dishonor entered the priestly government of Israel. Where there is dishonor, there is no glory. Glory and honor walk together.

HONOR PRECEDES GLORY

To shred what happened in Israel in those days we need to understand the meaning of the Hebrew word translated "glory." Understanding this, we will come to know what causes the loss of glory and where this loss begins.

The Hebrew term "Kabod" which is translated "glory", has the meaning of "weight" or "being heavy." This means that one only glorifies those who recognize the weight of their life or the weight of their authority. Therefore, the glory of God is incontestable, not only in the religious sphere but also outside it.

In the New Testament, the Greek term for glory is "doxa" (also written "doksa"). It appears approximately one hundred fifty-seven times. In texts like John 5:41, 44; John 8:54; 2 Corinthians 6: 8 and many others.

"I do not receive honor from men.
John 5:41 NKJV

In both texts use the word "doxa".

The word "kabod" that is translated as glory and that has the same sense of "heavy" or "weighing someone". Kabod is a derivative of kabed that is honor.

Kabed refers to the physical weight and kabod to the weight of importance that the person has. For example, God cannot be measured by its literal weight but by the weight of its importance to us. Kings were measured by the importance they had and should be honored for their position as rulers.

For that reason, some teachers and leaders generate doubt when they use the two words. Although honor and glory are very similar in meaning, they are different in their manifestation.

This difference is noticeable when the presence of God manifests. His presence is the deepest and most real glory that human beings can perceive, but to live this supernatural manifestation there is no other way than honor.

Honor leads to glory. You honor the one to whom you recognize that you have a weight over your life or an authority over you or your ministry. We honor someone important or who we depend on. When we depend on someone, all that he grants us, we return him by giving him the corresponding glory.

In the case of the priest Eli, he deserved a triple honor. He should be honored as a father, as a judge and as a high priest. His children never understood honor. They were fools.

Just as glory weighs for one who deserves honor, respect and admiration; in the same way honor is a very heavy burden for the fool. Who would think of honoring a fool?

> *As snow in summer and rain in harvest,*
> *So honor is not fitting for a fool.*
> *Proverbs 26:1 KNJV*

Like one who binds a stone in a sling
Is he who gives honor to a fool.
Proverbs 26:8 NKJV

THE OBJECTIVE OF HONOR AND GLORY WILL ALWAYS BE THE LORD

We must never lose sight of the fact that all attitudes of honor in our lives will reach the heart of the Lord. When I honor my brother, or my parents, or my bosses, or my pastors and leaders, the name of the Lord will always be glorified in each of these attitudes.

10 Be kindly affectionate to one another with brotherly love,
in honor giving preference to one another;
Romans 12:10 NKJV

Honor is part of the character of God's children. Seeking honor and glory for themselves is characteristic of the children of the world.

Our relationship with the heavenly Father must be protected on a platform of honor, fear and glory. It is impossible to walk with the Lord or with the Spirit without our honor sprouting in our hearts.

who alone has immortality, dwelling in unapproachable light, whom no man has seen or can see, to whom be honor and everlasting power. Amen.
1 Timothy 6:16 NKJV

For this One has been counted worthy of more glory than Moses, inasmuch as He who built the house has more honor than the house.
Hebrews 3:3 NKJV

"You are worthy, O Lord,
To receive glory and honor and power;
For You created all things,
And by Your will they exist and were created."
Revelations 4:11

saying with a loud voice:
"Worthy is the Lamb who was slain
To receive power and riches and wisdom,
And strength and honor and glory and blessing!"
13 And every creature which is in heaven and on the earth and under the earth and such as are in the sea, and all that are in them, I heard saying:
"Blessing and honor and glory and power
Be to Him who sits on the throne,
And to the Lamb, forever and ever!"
Revelations 5:12-13 NKJV

saying:

"Amen! Blessing and glory and wisdom,
Thanksgiving and honor and power and might,
Be to our God forever and ever.
Amen."
Revelations 7:12 NKJV

36 For of Him and through Him and to Him are all things, to whom be glory forever. Amen.
Romans 11:36 NKJV

We will examine in the next chapter what happened with the sons of the priest Eli, Phinehas and Hophni, who sinned and disobeyed their father's orders. Ministers of dishonor will always be foolish ministers.

CHAPTER 5

PHINEHAS AND HOPHNI: MINISTERS OF DISHONOR

22 Now Eli was very old; and he heard everything his sons did to all Israel, and how they lay with the women who assembled at the door of the tabernacle of meeting. 23 So he said to them, "Why do you do such things? For I hear of your evil dealings from all the people. 24 No, my sons! For it is not a good report that I hear. You make the Lord's people transgress. 25 If one man sins against another, God will judge him. But if a man sins against the Lord, who will intercede for him?" Nevertheless they did not heed the voice of their father, because the Lord desired to kill them.

26 And the child Samuel grew in stature, and in favor both with the Lord and men.

27 Then a man of God came to Eli and said to him, "Thus says the Lord: 'Did I not clearly reveal Myself to the house of your father when they were in Egypt in Pharaoh's house? 28 Did I not choose him out of all the tribes of Israel to be My priest, to offer upon My altar, to burn incense, and to wear an ephod before Me? And did I not give to the house of your father all the offerings of the children of Israel made by fire? 29 Why do you kick at My sacrifice and My offering which I have commanded in My dwelling place, and honor your sons more than Me, to make yourselves fat with the best of all the offerings of Israel My people?'

30 Therefore the Lord God of Israel says: 'I said indeed that your house and the house of your father would walk before Me forever.' But now the Lord says: 'Far be it from Me; for those who honor Me I will honor, and those who despise Me shall be lightly esteemed. 31 Behold, the days are coming that I will cut off your [c]arm and the arm of your father's house, so that there will not be an old man in your house. 32 And you will see an enemy in My dwelling place, despite all the good which God does for Israel. And there shall not be an old man in your house forever. 33 But any of your men whom I do not cut off from My altar shall consume your eyes and grieve your heart. And all the descendants of your house shall die in the flower of their age. 34 Now this shall be a sign to you that will come upon your two sons, on Hophni and Phinehas: in one day they shall die, both of them. 35 Then I will raise up for Myself a faithful priest who shall do according to what is in My heart and in My mind. I will build him a sure house, and he shall walk before My anointed forever. 36 And it shall come to pass that everyone who is left in your house will come and bow down to him for a piece of silver and a morsel of bread, and say, "Please, [d]put me in one of the priestly positions, that I may eat a piece of bread."
1 Samuel 2:22-36 NKJV

Eli's sons continually sinned by dishonoring the priesthood. The text states that they slept with the women who served at the door of the congregation (1 Samuel 2:22)

Eli rebuked them vigorously, but they did not listen to their father's voice, so God decided to kill them.

They died fighting the Philistines and Israel was defeated in battle and the Ark was captured by the Philistines. A soldier from the tribe of Benjamin came with the news to inform Eli what had happened. When he heard that the Philistines had captured the Ark, he fell back and died because he broke his neck.

His daughter-in-law, wife of Phinehas, had labor pains and gave birth to a child. Although the midwives tried to comfort her, she did not show much interest in the creature because her concern, like Eli's, was the loss of the Ark.

Before dying she called the child "Icabod", using the term "kabod" which means "glory." Icabod can mean "the glory of the Lord is gone" as well as "without glory." The Icabod expression meant that Israel had lost the Ark. Eli and his daughter-in-law worried about the Ark and not so much about the death of Hopni and Phinehas.

The Ark (the presence of the Lord; the glory of the Lord) was taken from Israel to the camp of the Philistines. Contrary to what certain poorly informed preachers claim, the glory (presence) of the Lord never departed from Israel. I explain myself: For Israel, the Ark was glory, presence, a motive of blessing and prosperity.

But what did the Ark represent to the Philistines? Struggles, tribulations, diseases and much suffering. It represented curse. Therefore, they had to return the Ark. Reading chapter 5 of the first book of Samuel, we will notice that where the Ark arrived, in Philistine villages and towns, it only left death, disease and misfortune. They were going from city to city until seven months later they decided to return it to Israel, where it would be a blessing.

DAGON WAS HUMILED BEFORE THE ARK

One of the greatest calamities suffered by the Philistines was to see their god Dagon humiliated before the Ark. Dagon was the power they worshiped and dared to put the Ark before their god. What they never imagined is to see their god the next day on the floor prostrated before the presence of the God of Israel.

> *2 When the Philistines took the ark of God, they brought it into the house of Dagon and set it by Dagon.*

3 And when the people of Ashdod arose early in the morning, there was Dagon, fallen on its face to the earth before the ark of the Lord. So they took Dagon and set it in its place again. 4 And when they arose early the next morning, there was Dagon, fallen on its face to the ground before the ark of the Lord. The head of Dagon and both the palms of its hands were broken off on the threshold; only Dagon's torso was left of it.
1 Samuel 5:2-4 NKJV

The glory of God is untouchable. No one can have an attitude of dishonor with the Lord and go unpunished. He never shares his glory with anyone. Glory is a divine exclusivity. By throwing the image of Dagon to the ground, the Lord placed it in a position of reverence and worship, showing the Philistines who the true God is.

THE DESHONRA OF PHINEHAS AND HOPHNI

Let's return to the sin of Phinehas and Hophni. When they exercised their priesthood under the authority of their father who was the high priest at that time. They were rebuked once (1 Samuel 2: 23-25) but did not obey their father. From there the Lord decided his death, according to verse 25.

By disobeying his father, he was dishonored. They did not give him the honor a son should give his father. In the Bible there are other stories of disobedience of children to their parents, but God did not decide to kill them. Why in this case was the Lord so hard on them?

Observe the fifth commandment in the Torah (Exodus 20:12). Simple disobedience to the father would already be reason enough for the Lord to shorten his days on earth.

12 "Honor your father and your mother, that your days may be long upon the land which the Lord your God is giving you.
Exodus 20:12 NKJV

The point is that Eli was their father, but he was also the high priest.

There was triple authority in Eli: Father, judge and priest. In what jurisdiction was disobedience performed? Was it at home, in the family or was it in the exercise of the priesthood? Take into account that at home Eli was only the head of his family, but as a high priest and judge he was responsible for all Israel, and therefore the spiritual father of the whole nation. He was a representative of the Lord and the official keeper of the Ark, that is, of the glory of God over all the people.

Remember that at that time the Kingdom of Israel had not yet been established. The priest was the highest authority. He also served as a judge.

Let me emphasize this issue of authority because I want you to understand that a triple authority also deserves a triple honor. Eli was father, judge and priest of Israel. Parental authority (family), legal authority (political/administrative) and spiritual authority (priesthood).

Without Authority, Without Honor.

This is an important lesson for today's religious leaders, who are ministers in the Church and are parents in their homes. They have the responsibility of double authority. It is a lesson for children too because they know that they have parental authority and spiritual authority.

Both must be obeyed. Both must be respected. Both must be honored.

Who reprimanded PHINEHAS AND HOPHNI? THE "ELI FATHER", THE "ELI JUDGE" OR THE "ELI PRIEST"?

Perhaps due to his advanced age, Eli no longer had enough energy to exercise discipline in the priestly body and therefore neglected diligence in his duties. He listened to the bad news and only felt sad for the testimony of his children.

In exhorting them, he positioned himself as a father. He was not at all bad because he possessed triple authority. If speaking to them as a father, they had repented, everything was fine and problem solved.

The problem is that the dishonor had so much in the character of Phinehas and Hophni that they did not respect him in any of the three authorities. We believe that if I had called your attention as a priest they might not have obeyed, and if I had done it as a judge either.

Dishonor is deaf. Dishonor is blind. Dishonor is cynical. Dishonor knows no limits. Dishonor is sarcastic. Dishonor is not afraid.

Compare the following verses:

22 Now Eli was very old; and he heard everything his sons did to all Israel, and how they lay with the women who assembled at the door of the tabernacle of meeting.
23 So he said to them, "Why do you do such things? For I hear of your evil dealings from all the people.

24 No, my sons! For it is not a good report that I hear. You make the Lord's people transgress. 25 If one man sins against another, God will judge him. But if a man sins against the Lord, who will intercede for him?" Nevertheless they did not heed the voice of their father, because the Lord desired to kill them.
1 Samuel 2:22-25 NKJV

Having reached the point that the Lord decided to kill them, it hardly mattered whether they obeyed or not.

The Lord was already communicating with him who would be the seed of honor in Israel to nullify all that shame practiced by the sons of Eli.

Samuel already heard, understood and obeyed the voice of the Lord. The Lord revealed to him his plans for who would assume Eli's place and restore Israel's honor to the peoples. The Bible teaches us that when God is going to do something on earth, he always reveals his plans to his prophets.

Surely the Lord God does nothing,
Unless He reveals His secret to His servants the prophets.
Amos 3:7 NKJV

And so God spoke with Samuel:

11 Then the Lord said to Samuel: "Behold, I will do something in Israel at which both ears of everyone who hears it will tingle. 12 In that day I will perform against Eli all that I have spoken concerning his house, from beginning to end. 13 For I have told him that I will judge his house forever for the iniquity which he knows, because his sons made themselves vile, and he did not restrain them. 14 And therefore I have sworn to the house of Eli that the iniquity of Eli's house shall not be atoned for by sacrifice or offering forever."
1 Samuel 3:11-14 NKJV

At first glance there seems to be a contradiction between the two texts. Eli rebuked his children, as stated in the first text. In the second he says that God had spoken several times with Eli; but he did not rebuke his children.

Understand the texts:
When Eli admonishes his children, he calls them MY CHILDREN. It is not about the priest calling the attention of his assistants, but about a father, with the heart of the father, exhorting his children. And that father was already 98 years old, very old, tired and blind.

Dishonor did not happen in Eli's house. Dishonor was in the House of God. Eli did not take good care of one or the other.

We will see repetition of similar events in the life of King David. When the Lord spoke with Samuel, he told him that he was going to discipline Eli's house. This refers to the priest who did not know or had no strength to discipline the priestly exercise that served as the basis and guardian of the glory of God in Israel.

When he heard the news of the death of his children, Eli showed no reaction, but upon hearing that the Ark had been taken by the Philistines, he fell back and broke his neck dying instantly (1 Samuel 4: 17-18)

The same happened with the wife of Phinehas, who had also been dishonored by her husband. Phinehas was an accomplished adulterer and did not respect her.

The news about the Ark shook her more than the death of her husband. Her last words were sad and disappointed by the fateful deeds. She named her son Icabod, in a prophetic reference about the loss of God's glory to the people.

THE SIN OF PHINEHAS AND HOPHNI

The sin of Phinehas and Hophni was to have dishonored the families (his family and those who came to bring offerings), the altar, the father, the government (judge), the priesthood and God.

In spite of everything, Eli left an interesting lesson, said: "If one man dishonors another, God will be the judge; But if you dishonor God, who can be a judge? Who can intercede for him?

HOW THE ROAD OF DISHONOR IS DEVELOPED

Notice how dishonor is a tragedy without limits in the life of the human being. Dishonor is producing children along the way. Dishonor is insatiable. With her you know that you are walking towards death, but you have no way to stop.

It is sad that there are Christians who live in disgrace, in the shortage and under the dominion of the spirit of misery. The saddest thing is that sometimes they defend their dishonorable posture using biblical verses that justify their failures and frustrations.

Hophni and his brother Phinehas followed the path of dishonor in the following order:

They stole the offering that was from the Lord They forgot the commitment to their ministry.

The fear disappeared giving rise to the lowest carnal instincts. In the verse below, we see the expression sons of Belial, the equivalent today of "sons of the devil".

Imagine two sons of the devil serving on the Altar of the Lord; or to these two subjects taking the Ark (the glory of the presence of the Lord) to the battlefield, to a war for which they were not prepared.

> *12 Now the sons of Eli were corrupt; they did not know the Lord. 13 And the priests' custom with the people was that when any man offered a sacrifice, the priest's servant would come with a three-pronged fleshhook in his hand while the meat was boiling. 14 Then he would thrust it into the pan, or kettle, or caldron, or pot; and the priest would take for himself all that the fleshhook brought up. So they did in Shiloh to all the Israelites who came there. 15 Also, before they burned the fat, the priest's servant would come and say to the man who sacrificed, "Give meat for roasting to the priest, for he will not take boiled meat from you, but raw."*
> *16 And if the man said to him, "They should really burn the fat first; then you may take as much as your heart desires," he would then answer him, "No, but you must give it now; and if not, I will take it by force."*

17 Therefore the sin of the young men was very great before the Lord, for men abhorred the offering of the Lord. 1 Samuel 2:12-17 NKJV

They slept with the women who came to offer, a sexual promiscuity practiced by pagan religions.

They implemented in Israel the practice of pagan nations that mixed religion with prostitution. They manipulated women by seducing them for the practice of carnal union, implying that it was pleasing to God.

They polluted the altar of the Lord. There was no more notion in them of what the profanity or profanity they incurred meant. The punishment could only be death. Sin in this case cannot be labeled "just" as adultery or fornication. The offense is deeper and that is what I try to demonstrate in this book.

The greatest evil in the history of these two young priests was dishonor, not punctual sins such as robbery, prostitution, hypocrisy, disobedience, etc.

Dishonor unleashed all the punishment that came immediately and then to all his offspring.

> *Now Eli was very old; and he heard everything his sons did to all Israel, and how they lay with the women who assembled at the door of the tabernacle of meeting.*
> *1 Samuel 2:22 NKJV*

The Ark of the Lord could only be taken into battle if the Lord himself ordered it. To move the Ark, one must observe a whole ritual prescribed in the Torah.

The spiritual moment in Israel was not the best but on the contrary it was a time of dishonor. So, boldness came to those responsible for such dishonor. They paid with their life and the loss of the Ark.

> *And when the people had come into the camp, the elders of Israel said, "Why has the Lord defeated us today before the Philistines? Let us bring the ark of the covenant of the Lord from Shiloh to us, that when it comes among us it may save us from the hand of our enemies."*
> *4 So the people sent to Shiloh, that they might bring from there the ark of the covenant of the Lord of hosts, who dwells between the cherubim. And the two sons of Eli, Hophni and Phinehas, were there with the ark of the covenant of God.*
> *1 Samuel 4:3-4 NKJV*

Relaxed and dishonest priests, adulterous and unfaithful husbands, disobedient sons to the father and bad guardians of the Ark of the Covenant who lost it to the enemies.

One dishonor after another, unbridled madness and without limits.

WEEKING UNREASES GENERATIONAL CURSE

The punishment of dishonor: Death, generational curse and misery

Dishonor activates the curse on the offspring of those who practiced it. This sentence was initially uttered in the Garden of Eden by the Lord when he went to visit Adam and Eve after sin.

> *14 So the Lord God said to the serpent:*
> *"Because you have done this,*
> *You are cursed more than all cattle,*
> *And more than every beast of the field;*
> *On your belly you shall go,*
> *And you shall eat dust*
> *All the days of your life.*
> *15 And I will put enmity*
> *Between you and the woman,*
> *And between your seed and her Seed;*

He shall bruise your head,
And you shall bruise His heel."
16 To the woman He said:
"I will greatly multiply your sorrow and your conception;
In pain you shall bring forth children;
Your desire shall be for your husband,
And he shall rule over you."
17 Then to Adam He said, "Because you have heeded the voice of your wife, and have eaten from the tree of which I commanded you, saying, 'You shall not eat of it':
"Cursed is the ground for your sake;
In toil you shall eat of it
All the days of your life.
18 Both thorns and thistles it shall bring forth for you,
And you shall eat the herb of the field.
19 In the sweat of your face you shall eat bread
Till you return to the ground,
For out of it you were taken;
For dust you are,
And to dust you shall return."
Genesis 3:14-19 NKJV

In chapter 4 of Genesis we find the Lord again punishing Cain and talking about his offspring and his death.

Then the Lord said to Cain, "Where is Abel your brother?"

*He said, "I do not know. Am I my brother's keeper?"
10 And He said, "What have you done? The voice of your brother's blood cries out to Me from the ground. 11 So now you are cursed from the earth, which has opened its mouth to receive your brother's blood from your hand. 12 When you till the ground, it shall no longer yield its strength to you. A fugitive and a vagabond you shall be on the earth."
13 And Cain said to the Lord, "My punishment is greater than I can bear! 14 Surely You have driven me out this day from the face of the ground; I shall be hidden from Your face; I shall be a fugitive and a vagabond on the earth, and it will happen that anyone who finds me will kill me."
15 And the Lord said to him, "Therefore, whoever kills Cain, vengeance shall be taken on him sevenfold." And the Lord set a mark on Cain, lest anyone finding him should kill him.
Genesis 4:9-15 NKJV*

Cain became the symbol of a generation of dishonor. He became terribly famous for killing his own brother driven by a clumsy motive.

1.   The death of the ministers of dishonor

In that battle, the presence of God did not bring victory to his people.

The truth is that the Lord did not want to be there. He sent a spirit of death that attacked in general. 30,000 men from Israel died on the battlefield. When the messenger came to Silo to report the defeat of Israel, the high priest Eli died. His daughter-in-law, wife of Phinehas, suffered labor pains and died as well.

> *Also the ark of God was captured; and the two sons of Eli, Hophni and Phinehas, died.*
> *1 Samuel 4:11-15 NKJV*

2.   The Generational Curse

That spirit of death came to live in the descendants of Eli through the dishonor of his children. See the divine sentence in the verses below: There will be no more elders in your house, that is, everyone will die in youth.

> *30 Therefore the Lord God of Israel says: 'I said indeed that your house and the house of your father would walk before Me forever.' But now the Lord says: 'Far be it from Me; for those who honor Me I will honor, and those who despise Me shall be lightly esteemed.*
> *31 Behold, the days are coming that I will cut off your arm and the arm of your father's house, so that there will not be an old man in your house.*

32 And you will see an enemy in My dwelling place, despite all the good which God does for Israel. And there shall not be an old man in your house forever. 33 But any of your men whom I do not cut off from My altar shall consume your eyes and grieve your heart. And all the descendants of your house shall die in the flower of their age.
1 Samuel 2:30-33 NKJV

3.   Poverty and Misery

Scarcity and misery go hand in hand with dishonor. God's judgment is severe with dishonor. They stole from the altar of the Lord. They got fed up with the fatness of the sacrifices that didn't belong to them. Their offspring would have a shortage of what they had in abundance dishonestly.

His offspring would ask for alms. They would beg for a piece of bread and beg for any small work in the priesthood not to starve to death. The curse generated by dishonor is cruel.

And it shall come to pass that everyone who is left in your house will come and bow down to him for a piece of silver and a morsel of bread, and say,
"Please, put me in one of the priestly positions, that I may eat a piece of bread." "
1 Samuel 2:36 NKJV

4. The dishonored will live at the expense of the honest

The restorer of the honor of the priestly ministry would now be the high priest who would take the place of the old leader, who did not fight corruption and who did not honor the house of the Lord.

Then I will raise up for Myself a faithful priest who shall do according to what is in My heart and in My mind. I will build him a sure house, and he shall walk before My anointed forever.
1 Samuel 2:35 NKJV

Samuel was being trained by God to place the name and presence of the Lord in the heart of the people again in a holy and reverent manner.

And it shall come to pass that everyone who is left in your house will come and bow down to him for a piece of silver and a morsel of bread, and say, "Please, put me in one of the priestly positions, that I may eat a piece of bread." "'
1 Samuel 2:36 NKJV

The ministers of honor are those who keep the riches of the Lord and administer them. Those who live in dishonor do not have that privilege. That is why they will always have to go from those honest lords who have the keys of the Kingdom of heaven and receive special revelations from the Lord.

The faithful priest referred to in verse 35 belongs to the lineage of the ministers of honor.

CHAPTER 6

HONOR ESTABLISHES US IN OUR PROPHETIC DESTINATION

Every man or woman of God has a position in the Kingdom of God that we call our position or our prophetic destiny.

When we are born, God has in our hands our fully formed history. He predestined us to fulfill his purposes with us.

God does not create us by chance or just because He did not have anything else to do. He has control of what He wants on earth. Therefore, we are born with a definite purpose. Although we do not previously know that purpose, it does not mean that we can live according to the circumstances of this life.

A wise God does not work without a plan. He knows what he does, always. We must understand that nobody is born in the wrong place or out of time.

14 I will praise You, for I am fearfully and wonderfully made;
Marvelous are Your works,
And that my soul knows very well.
15 My frame was not hidden from You,
When I was made in secret,

And skillfully wrought in the lowest parts of the earth.
16 Your eyes saw my substance, being yet unformed.
And in Your book they all were written,
The days fashioned for me,
When as yet there were none of them.
Psalms 139:14-16 NKJV

Sin, the absence of God's presence in our lives, worldly pleasures and even the obsession to achieve success lead us to a life of dishonor, far from the foundations of honor established by the Lord. That set of conjunctures and facts in our life lead us to live far from our real purpose established and decreed by God to establish us in the correct prophetic position within his Kingdom.

If you live a life without honor, do not expect success or the blessings of the Most-High. He first positions you and then blesses you.

HONOR FILLED ACTIONS SET YOU UP FOR HONOR POSITION

The attractive story of an unhappy prostitute destined to die

When Joshua sent spies to collect information about the city of Jericho, its soldiers and its military weapons; The two Israelites, after being noticed in the city, decided to enter the house of a woman named Rahab, a well-known prostitute in the city. Their decision was intelligent, because entering a brothel they would not call the attention of the people so much.

But someone saw them enter Rahab's house and spread the word. Then the messengers of the king of Jericho arrived to inquire about the two men. Rahab lied to the king's emissaries saying that the men had really been there but that they had already left. The truth is that they were hidden on the roof under the bunches of linen stored there.

Now Joshua the son of Nun sent out two men from Acacia Grove to spy secretly, saying, "Go, view the land, especially Jericho." So they went, and came to the house of a harlot named Rahab, and lodged there. 2 And it was told the king of Jericho, saying, "Behold, men have come here tonight from the children of Israel to search out the country."

So the king of Jericho sent to Rahab, saying, "Bring out the men who have come to you, who have entered your house, for they have come to search out all the country."
Joshua 2:1-3 NKJV

We all have two seeds: that of honor and that of dishonor
Rahab never imagined that his life would be transformed by the activation of the wise divine plan whose outcome would be to take it towards his prophetic destiny.

Some unbelievers would call that luck or mere fatality working in their favor.

From that meeting, there was a succession of words, successes and commitments between her and the two Israelites, all settling under the mantle of honor. This is a beautiful story. Without commitment to honor, the pact would not come to a happy ending.

Rahab saw the fact of protecting Joshua's two spies as an opportunity to change his life. Immediately that the king's soldiers left his house, she made a request to the spies, in the form of a pact, to change their destiny. In chapter 1 we show that glory and honor always walk together.
Rahab the prostitute, a woman who lived in dishonor, had within her the seed of honor.

Glory walks with honor.

Rahab did not know the foundation of honor yet; but he had the seed of honor within himself. She did not know the honor due to Jehovah; but he knew the glory of the Lord's deeds and feared him for what he had heard about his power and his strength. Because he knew the glory of God, it was easy for him to present the petition that would change his life forever and establish it in his prophetic destiny.

She was humble talking about Jehovah's deeds with her people and said she knew of his greatness and also of his mercy.
See his proposal, which worked as a key that unlocked his future:

Now before they lay down, she came up to them on the roof, 9 and said to the men: "I know that the Lord has given you the land, that the terror of you has fallen on us, and that all the inhabitants of the land are fainthearted because of you. 10 For we have heard how the Lord dried up the water of the Red Sea for you when you came out of Egypt, and what you did to the two kings of the Amorites who were on the other side of the Jordan, Sihon and Og, whom you utterly destroyed.

> *11 And as soon as we heard these things, our hearts melted; neither did there remain any more courage in anyone because of you, for the Lord your God, He is God in heaven above and on earth beneath.*

12 Now therefore, I beg you, swear to me by the Lord, since I have shown you kindness, that you also will show kindness to my father's house, and give me a true token, 13 and spare my father, my mother, my brothers, my sisters, and all that they have, and deliver our lives from death."
Joshua 2:8-13 NKJV

Joshua's envoys accepted her request and swore to Rahab that the covenant would be fulfilled if she honored his part of the agreement.

So the men answered her, "Our lives for yours, if none of you tell this business of ours. And it shall be, when the Lord has given us the land, that we will deal kindly and truly with you." 15 Then she let them down by a rope through the window, for her house was on the city wall; she dwelt on the wall. 16 And she said to them, "Get to the mountain, lest the pursuers meet you. Hide there three days, until the pursuers have returned. Afterward you may go your way."

17 So the men said to her: "We will be blameless of this oath of yours which you have made us swear,
18 unless, when we come into the land, you bind this line of scarlet cord in the window through which you let us down, and unless you bring your father, your mother, your brothers, and all your father's household to your own home.

*19 So it shall be that whoever goes outside the doors of your house into the street, his blood shall be on his own head, and we will be guiltless. And whoever is with you in the house, his blood shall be on our head if a hand is laid on him.
20 And if you tell this business of ours, then we will be free from your oath which you made us swear."
Joshua 2:14-20 NKJV*

Remember that in Chapter 2 we mentioned, in the article that talks about the sanctions of dishonor, that there is a GENERAL CURSE for those who practice dishonor.

Here in this text that tells the story of Rahab, it is the opposite, the practice of honor establishes the GENERATIONAL BLESSING.

Until his encounter with the two Israelites in his house, Rahab was the shame of his entire family. It was the disgrace of the family. She brought the curse of prostitution to her generations. What future would the women of Rahab's house have? What daughter is pleased to say: My mother is a prostitute? What granddaughter talks with her friends and says: I am a granddaughter of a prostitute?

In Rahab the seed of honor changed her prophetic destiny and her generation.

In the negotiation with the spies she included her father, her mother, her brothers, her sisters and all her relatives. She went a little further and also included all her assets. She saved the people and everything they had.

> *Now therefore, I beg you, swear to me by the Lord, since I have shown you kindness, that you also will show kindness to my father's house, and give me a true token, 13 and spare my father, my mother, my brothers, my sisters, and all that they have, and deliver our lives from death."*
> *Joshua 2:12-13 NKJV*

Joshua honored the word of his officers and after the victory over Jericho, he sent for Rahab and all his family with his property and protected them by taking them to live with those of Israel.

> *Now the city shall be doomed by the Lord to destruction, it and all who are in it. Only Rahab the harlot shall live, she and all who are with her in the house, because she hid the messengers that we sent.*
> *Joshua 2:17 NKJV*

> *But Joshua had said to the two men who had spied out the country, "Go into the harlot's house, and from there bring out the woman and all that she has, as you swore to her."*

> *23 And the young men who had been spies went in and brought out Rahab, her father, her mother, her brothers, and all that she had. So they brought out all her relatives and left them outside the camp of Israel.*
> *Joshua 6:22-23 NKJV*

> *And Joshua spared Rahab the harlot, her father's household, and all that she had. So she dwells in Israel to this day, because she hid the messengers whom Joshua sent to spy out Jericho.*
> *Joshua 6:25 NKJV*

Something interesting in Rahab's life. She was a prostitute in Jericho but being adopted by the Israelites left that promiscuous life behind. In Israel prostitution was not seen with good eyes. On the contrary, there was a radical stance on the merits.

When accepted by the Israelites, Rahab was established by the Lord in his prophetic destiny. He left dishonor behind and changed the story of all his offspring. He came out of the curse toward the blessing.

See the expression in the last verse of the text cited above: Thus, Joshua gave life to the prostitute Rahab ("But Joshua saved Rahab the harlot" RV).

If Joshua gave life to Rahab, it is because she had no life. In Jericho, what I expected was death. Joshua delivered her from death, drawing her to life. He brought her out of dishonor and brought her to honor.

Ascension, honor and grace over Rahab's life
Once integrated with the Israelite people, their life takes a new direction. His prophetic destiny begins to be designed.

A marriage to a Jew named Salmon led her to integrate the genealogy of Jesus. From that marriage was born his son Boaz who married Ruth and fathered Obed, who fathered Jesse, who was the father of King David.

Ram begot Amminadab, Amminadab begot Nahshon, and Nahshon begot Salmon. 5 Salmon begot Boaz by Rahab, Boaz begot Obed by Ruth, Obed begot Jesse, 6 and Jesse begot David the king.

David the king begot Solomon by her who had been the wife of Uriah.
Matthew 1:4-6 NKJV

Honor sets you in your prophetic destiny.

The woman destined to die in a few days later with her whole family, changes her destiny and becomes the mother of blessed generations. In these blessed generations the Messiah is born that would change the history of mankind.

Honor changes our generational destiny. Dishonor destroys our generational destiny.

RUT LA MOABITA, ANOTHER CASE OF HONOR AND PROPHETIC DESTINATION

The story of Ruth, the Moabite, is another episode in the Bible of changing prophetic destiny.

This young woman married a Jew named Mahlon, son of Elimelek with his wife Naomi. Kilion, Mahlon's brother, married Orpah.

After about ten years, Elimelek died leaving Naomi a widow. Sometime later their children also die leaving the daughters-in-law in the same widowhood situation.

With the critical situation for all three, Naomi decided to return to Israel. Her daughters-in-law decide to accompany her, so she won't be alone. At first, she refused and advised them to stay in their land because they had no obligation to return with her.

Orpah returned to Moab, but Ruth did not want to stay but was determined to accompany Naomi.

But Ruth said:
"Entreat me not to leave you,
Or to turn back from following after you;
For wherever you go, I will go;
And wherever you lodge, I will lodge;
Your people shall be my people,
And your God, my God.
17 Where you die, I will die,
And there will I be buried.
The Lord do so to me, and more also,
If anything but death parts you and me."
Ruth 1: 16-17 NKJV

This was done. They returned to Israel. The Moabite decided to live with the Jews. She did not abandon her mother-in-law but took care of her. The love she had for her husband became an honor for her mother-in-law.

What is the origin of Ruth, the Moabite?
We will know the origin of the Moabites and see the language of this woman and the inhabitants of Moab.

Then Lot went up out of Zoar and dwelt in the mountains, and his two daughters were with him; for he was afraid to dwell in Zoar. And he and his two daughters dwelt in a cave.
31 Now the firstborn said to the younger, "Our father is old, and there is no man on the earth to come in to us as is the custom of all the earth.
32 Come, let us make our father drink wine, and we will lie with him, that we may preserve the lineage of our father."
33 So they made their father drink wine that night. And the firstborn went in and lay with her father, and he did not know when she lay down or when she arose.
34 It happened on the next day that the firstborn said to the younger, "Indeed I lay with my father last night; let us make him drink wine tonight also, and you go in and lie with him, that we may preserve the [b]lineage of our father."
35 Then they made their father drink wine that night also. And the younger arose and lay with him, and he did not know when she lay down or when she arose.
36 Thus both the daughters of Lot were with child by their father.
37 The firstborn bore a son and called his name Moab; he is the father of the Moabites to this day.
38 And the younger, she also bore a son and called his name Ben-Ammi; he is the father of the people of Ammon to this day.
Genesis 19-30-38 NKJV

The Moabites were descendants of Lot's incestuous relationship with his eldest daughter.

Notice that she lied, manipulated and accomplished her mission. That evil feature of his character was the presence of these demons that accompanied their descendants throughout their lives. He dominated his father and manipulated his sister. She lied when she said there were no men on earth. His father's uncle, Abraham, had a great town with him. In addition, there were other towns in that region.

Ruth came from a genealogy of dishonor. There was a divine order in the Torah about the Moabites. Never be part of the Israelite people. Neither enter nor worship.

"One of illegitimate birth shall not enter the assembly of the Lord; even to the tenth generation none of his descendants shall enter the assembly of the Lord.

"An Ammonite or Moabite shall not enter the assembly of the Lord; even to the tenth generation none of his descendants shall enter the assembly of the Lord forever,
Deuteronomy 23:2-3 NKJV

The honor that Ruth gave to Naomi, took her out of the genealogy of dishonor and led her to the generation of honor. He changed his prophetic destiny.

In Israel, he met Boaz, through Naomi, and married him. They had a son they called Obed. This Obed was the father of Jesse, who was the father of David, King David.

See the difference in the attitude of honor. The foreign widow enters Israel and becomes her grandmother of King David. As a consequence, it also enters the lineage of Jesus Christ.

He changed his life and changed the destiny of his generations. You can do that too. Enter the honor and live in the honor. That way you will only have victory. You and yours.

Living an honest life is not an option, it is a divine order.

> Honor all people. Love the brotherhood. Fear God. Honor the king.
> 1 Peter 2:17 NKJV

Chapter 7

THE WAR OF THE TWO GENERATIONS
Introduction

God created a generation to inhabit the earth. Sin was responsible for dividing this generation into two. From the moment the man knew good and evil he had to choose and determine which path to follow. From the beginning it has been like that.

The Lord did not want two enemy generations living in the same world, since his creation was destined for honor. Adam and his family were not created to dwell in a dimension of dishonor. Life in Eden was a way of life that he received from the Eternal, a divine culture, based on the foundations of honor.

They lived in perfect harmony and spiritual integration, in an environment in which evil had no place.

With disobedience the door of knowledge of evil was opened, and with evil all the perversities generated in the dimension of evil entered to include, of course, dishonor.

The first victims of dishonor by divine order were Adam and his family, knowing the punishments from their attitude.

14 So the Lord God said to the serpent:

"Because you have done this,
You are cursed more than all cattle,
And more than every beast of the field;
On your belly you shall go,
And you shall eat dust
All the days of your life.
15 And I will put enmity
Between you and the woman,
And between your seed and her Seed;
He shall bruise your head,
And you shall bruise His heel."
16 To the woman He said:
"I will greatly multiply your sorrow and your conception;
In pain you shall bring forth children;
Your desire shall be for your husband,
And he shall rule over you."
17 Then to Adam He said, "Because you have heeded the voice of your wife, and have eaten from the tree of which I commanded you, saying, 'You shall not eat of it':
"Cursed is the ground for your sake;
In toil you shall eat of it
All the days of your life.
18 Both thorns and thistles it shall bring forth for you,
And you shall eat the herb of the field.
19 In the sweat of your face you shall eat bread

Till you return to the ground,
For out of it you were taken;
For dust you are,
And to dust you shall return."
Genesis 3:14-19 NKJV

The expulsion from the Garden of Eden was the most terrible sentence because with it he was losing his place of contact with the presence of the Eternal. The price of dishonor is very high. Adam experienced this price in his own life.

Another detail that we should not ignore is that the same Lord who created everything had to release the curse on man and nature.

The door of dishonor, which brought so much harm to man, was opened and would reach humanity for all its existence, until Christ came to earth to show us the door of honor and guided us to enter in.

Two Brothers, Children Of The Same Parents: Two Enemy Generations

In the event of Cain and Abel, the division into two generations occurred: that of honor and that of dishonor.

From there the two entered into conflict that will only end with the Second Coming of Christ.

In chapter 4 of the book of Genesis we find five significant events:

The first two offerings;
The first three homicides occurred in the history of mankind;
The beginning of the industry;
The first bigamy;
A destitution and a restoration.
Let's see what happened on that day.

1.   Dishonor In The First Offering

Now Adam knew Eve his wife, and she conceived and bore Cain, and said, "I have acquired a man from the Lord."
2 Then she bore again, this time his brother Abel. Now Abel was a keeper of sheep, but Cain was a tiller of the ground.
3 And in the process of time it came to pass that Cain brought an offering of the fruit of the ground to the Lord.
4 Abel also brought of the firstborn of his flock and of their fat. And the Lord respected Abel and his offering,
5 but He did not respect Cain and his offering. And Cain was very angry, and his countenance fell.
Genesis 4:1-5 NKJV

It is good to remember that these offerings were Adam's teachings to his children.

It was a prophetic offering pointing towards the sacrifice of Christ, because the parents ministered on the seed that would step on the head of the serpent.

A)   Abel's Offering

The Bible mentions that Abel was a shepherd. The fruits of his work were the animals with which he lived. When bringing his offering, he presented an immaculate lamb, without spot or defect. A perfect animal
His offering was accepted by God.

B)   Cain's Offering

Cain for his part was a farmer of the field. He dealt with the things of the earth. He decided to bring to the Lord the fruit of his work, believing that it brought a perfect offering. God rejected it and rebuked him because he was angry. Why did God reject his offering?

Notice what it says in Genesis 3, verses 17 and 18:

17 Then to Adam He said, "Because you have heeded the voice of your wife, and have eaten from the tree of which I commanded you, saying, 'You shall not eat of it':
"Cursed is the ground for your sake;
In toil you shall eat of it
All the days of your life.
18 Both thorns and thistles it shall bring forth for you,
And you shall eat the herb of the field.
Genesis 3:17-18

Cain brought to the altar of the Lord fruits of a cursed earth, fruits that bear curse seeds. How can anyone think of giving God things that come from cursing?

What option did Cain have?

If the offering was prophetic, pointing to the "seed of the woman" that was Jesus Christ, it must have been a blood offering. The lamb in Abel's sacrifice taught his generations what Christ would one day do.

Cain had discomfort in his heart because he didn't have a sheep for the honor offering. He had fruits of the land he worked with. He could have made some exchange with his brother who had many animals.

Cain had no wisdom, or lacked humility, to ask his brother for an animal to offer to the Lord. If he didn't want to ask, he could have bought some animal for the sacrifice.

Perhaps for these reasons he decided to offer the Lord anything. I can guarantee that offering "anything" to the Lord is pure dishonor.

He went to the altar with his heart disturbed because he knew that Abel was doing the right thing and he was wrong. He was fully aware of what he was doing but he still did it.

People of dishonor do not usually measure the weight of their actions. Even today we have within the churches a generation of dishonor that proclaim that God accepts anything. They say he accepts anything if it's done from the heart.

If you hear someone talk like that, know that is a person who does not know what honor is. God wants you to give what he asks, not what you want to give. It is he who works in us so wanting as doing.

for it is God who works in you both to will and to do for His good pleasure.
Philippians 2:13 NKJV

Of Adam, God asked obedience. Noah was asked to build an Ark. To Abraham He asked for his son. To Moses, to take his people out of Egypt. To Joshua, to take the promised land and distribute it to his people. To Gideon, who defended Israel from the Midianites.

To Ana, a sterile woman, to give her a child. Samuel was determined by the moral restoration of the priesthood in Israel.

To David, the worship and government of Israel. María, José's wife, was asked to borrow the uterus. To Joseph, Mary's husband, who assumed the earthly fatherhood of Jesus. Jesus determined the cross.

To the apostles, who took the word of Jerusalem to the ends of the world. Paul was determined to suffer for his name. To Juan, to show the world how things would be at the end of time.

All these, and many more in the Bible, honored God with what he determined for each one. This is honor.

Dishonor is that you try to "endorse" the Lord what you think will please you.

2. The first crime, its importance in the subject of honor

A.   Reasons for Abel's Death

There are many preachers who emphasize Abel's death as a result of Cain's jealousy. This trivializes the matter between the two brothers. When Cain calls his brother to the field, there was nothing between them. Abel had done nothing against Cain. They had not fought or had any misunderstanding. There seemed to be peace between them. Therefore, Abel did not contract to go to the field. There he was cowardly killed by Cain. Notice one tremendous thing: Cain, representing dishonor, killed Abel, representative of honor.

Read the text of 1 John 3:12:

> *not as Cain who was of the wicked one and murdered his brother. And why did he murder him? Because his works were evil and his brother's righteous.*

B. A Generation Killing Another Generation

If he paid attention to the text quoted above, he knows why he killed him? Because his works (those of Cain) were bad. They were works of dishonor. Instead those of his brother, Abel, were fair. They were works of honor.

The truth is that we see one generation destroying another. Do you know what happened since that day? There was no more generation of honor to worship God. Abel's generation did not continue but Cain's did. The generation of honor died, that of dishonor survived and multiplied.

From this event, the generations of misfortune always persecute and want to destroy the generations of honor.

3. The Consequences of Punishment

A.   Punishment And Its Implications

9 Then the Lord said to Cain, "Where is Abel your brother?" I said, "I do not know. Am I my brother's keeper?" 10 And He said, "What have you done? The voice of your brother's blood cries out to Me from the ground. 11 So now you are cursed from the earth, which has opened its mouth to receive your brother's blood from your hand. 12 When you till the ground, it shall no longer yield its strength to you. A fugitive and a vagabond you shall be on the earth." 13 And Cain said to the Lord, "My punishment is greater than I can bear!

*14 Surely You have driven me out this day from the face of the ground; I shall be hidden from Your face; I shall be a fugitive and a vagabond on the earth, and it will happen that anyone who finds me will kill me."
15 And the Lord said to him, "Therefore, whoever kills Cain, vengeance shall be taken on him sevenfold." And the Lord set a mark on Cain, lest anyone finding him should kill him.
Genesis 4:9-16 NKJV*

The Family of Cain

16 Then Cain went out from the presence of the Lord and dwelt in the land of Nod on the east of Eden.

Cain's generation is cursed, and the earth would be barren, denying him the sustenance he gave everyone. He was afraid imagining that he would be killed because of his crime.

When the Bible mentions that he would be avenged seven times, for a matter of interpretation the punishment was multiplied by seven. Actually, the original text says that he would be avenged in the seventh generation, not seven times.

B. The death of Cain in the seventh generation
When Cain left, the Bible says that he took a wife and went to dwell in the land of Nod.

Cain's generation is cursed, and the earth would be barren, denying him the sustenance he gave everyone. He was afraid imagining that he would be killed because of his crime.

When the Bible mentions that he would be avenged seven times, for a matter of interpretation the punishment was multiplied by seven. Actually, the original text says that he would be avenged in the seventh generation, not seven times.

B. The death of Cain in the seventh generation

When Cain left, the Bible says that he took a wife and went to dwell in the land of Nod.
Genesis 4:16 NKJV

He married and had a son whom he called Enoch. Thus, begins the seven generations of Cain:

17 And Cain knew his wife, and she conceived and bore Enoch. And he built a city, and called the name of the city after the name of his son—Enoch.
18 To Enoch was born Irad; and Irad begot Mehujael, and Mehujael begot Methushael, and Methushael begot Lamech.
19 Then Lamech took for himself two wives: the name of one was Adah, and the name of the second was Zillah.

20 And Adah bore Jabal. He was the father of those who dwell in tents and have livestock. 21 His brother's name was Jubal. He was the father of all those who play the harp and [a]flute. 22 And as for Zillah, she also bore Tubal-Cain, an instructor of every craftsman in bronze and iron. And the sister of Tubal-Cain was Naamah.
Genesis 4:17-22 NKJV

Observe The Seven Generations:

Enoch
Irad
Mehujael
Methushael
Lamech
Jubal
Tubal-Cain

In a hunt, Lamec meets Cain and without recognizing him kills him, a young man who was with him was also killed. Dishonor is still present in the generation of Cain. According to the word of God, he was killed in the seventh generation.

Although the one who killed him was Lamec, they were already living the seventh generation because Jubal, son of Lamec with Ada, was the sixth generation.

Tubal-Cain son of Lamec with Zila was the seventh generation.

4. Restoration of the generation of honor
At this point, Eve had another son.

25 And Adam knew his wife again, and she bore a son and named him Seth, "For God has appointed another seed for me instead of Abel, whom Cain killed." 26 And as for Seth, to him also a son was born; and he named him Enosh. Then men began to call on the name of the Lord.
Genesis 4:25-26

Notice that Eve testifies that the son she had now, Set, went instead of Abel. It is clear that Eve after Abel's death had other children; but in this case she affirms that this son came to be instead of Abel. It was the generation of honor that was being born and being restored. It was from the son of Seth, named Enos, that they began to invoke the name of the Lord. Again, the honor generation was restored.

The problem is that now the two generations began to coexist and lock in a real war.

5. Christ identified the two generations in the church

When Jesus began his ministry and revealed the model of what the Church would be like, he said that within the same flock there would be wheat and tares, that is, those who honor and those who dishonor.

"Then the servants of the householder came and said to him, Lord, did you not sow good seed in your field? Where, then, does it have tares?

27 So the servants of the owner came and said to him, 'Sir, did you not sow good seed in your field? How then does it have tares?' 28 He said to them, 'An enemy has done this.' The servants said to him, 'Do you want us then to go and gather them up?' 29 But he said, 'No, lest while you gather up the tares you also uproot the wheat with them. 30 Let both grow together until the harvest, and at the time of harvest I will say to the reapers, "First gather together the tares and bind them in bundles to burn them, but gather the wheat into my barn."'

Matthew 13:27-30 NKJV

In another text, he calls them sheep and kids.

"When the Son of Man comes in His glory, and all the holy angels with Him, then He will sit on the throne of His glory. 32 All the nations will be gathered before Him, and He will separate them one from another, as a shepherd divides his sheep from the goats.

33 And He will set the sheep on His right hand, but the goats on the left. 34 Then the King will say to those on His right hand, 'Come, you blessed of My Father, inherit the kingdom prepared for you from the foundation of the world:
Matthew 25:31-34 NKJV

The churches live with the two generations in their temples.

At this time, in any church, the pastor will always be shepherding a generation of honor and another of dishonor. Sheep and kids. Faithful and unfaithful. Unfortunately, we do not have enough discernment to separate one generation from the other.

This truth may seem cruel; but there is no way around it. Imagine that you have to accept that a part of the people you pastor will go to hell, and you don't have how to avoid it or how to change this harsh spiritual sentence.

Many times, a local leader orders a minister of the generation of dishonor. With all certainty in the future this minister will give him a lot of work. He lives in dishonor and if he becomes a minister, he is a minister of dishonor.

Order ministers of honor and you will always have faithful ministers by your side.

The Apostle Paul Spoke Of The Vessels Of Honor

In writing to Timothy, Paul prophesied about the last days and with extraordinary precision he identified the type of people who would walk through the churches at the end of time:

But know this, that in the last days perilous times will come:
2 For men will be lovers of themselves, lovers of money, boasters, proud, blasphemers, disobedient to parents, unthankful, unholy, 3 unloving, unforgiving, slanderers, without self-control, brutal, despisers of good,
4 traitors, headstrong, haughty, lovers of pleasure rather than lovers of God,
5 having a form of godliness but denying its power. And from such people turn away!
6 For of this sort are those who creep into households and make captives of gullible women loaded down with sins, led away by various lusts,
7 always learning and never able to come to the knowledge of the truth.
8 Now as Jannes and Jambres resisted Moses, so do these also resist the truth: men of corrupt minds, disapproved concerning the faith;
9 but they will progress no further, for their folly will be manifest to all, as theirs also was.
2 Timothy 3:1-9 NKJV

Do you know how many negative adjectives mentioning sinners are in this text? Twenty-three adjectives showing the character of a generation that would live in churches in recent times.
It is the generation of dishonor trying to kill the generation of honor. In an earlier chapter, Paul mentions the vessels of honor and the vessels of dishonor.

> *19 Nevertheless the solid foundation of God stands, having this seal: "The Lord knows those who are His," and, "Let everyone who names the name of Christ depart from iniquity."*
> *20 But in a great house there are not only vessels of gold and silver, but also of wood and clay, some for honor and some for dishonor.*
> *21 Therefore if anyone cleanses himself from the latter, he will be a vessel for honor, sanctified and useful for the Master, prepared for every good work.*
> *2 Timothy 2:19-21 NKJV*

Paul knew the matter very well because of the countless churches he had passed through and he knew as none the character of one who loves God and one who does not love him. He knew what a glass of honor and a glass of dishonor was.

What generation do you belong to? If I were in the wrong generation, there is still time to change.

CHAPTER 8

DISHONOR DESTROYS YOUR PROPHETIC DESTINATION

In chapter 3 we talk about honor restoring your prophetic destiny. Here we are going to comment on the disaster that dishonor brings to the lives of the men and women of God. Dishonor begins sweeping the person responsible for dishonor and then persecutes his generations.

In the examples we are going to give, you will observe that dishonor develops the same process of honor. Just as honor positions you in your prophetic destiny and grows day after day, manifesting the favors of the Lord over all that concerns you; that is, family life, ministerial, financial, and then move towards your offspring. Dishonor travels through the same process.

HONOR ATTRACTS BLESSING, DISHONOR DEATRACTS BLESSING

Honor will leave powerful traces that will affect your story throughout your life and after your death, she will shout your name to those who did not know you. Those who did not know you will respect and love you.

Dishonor on the contrary, will leave deep scars that destroy you here and reproduce for your offspring.

Those who did not know you will make fun of you and discredit you.

Honor produces profits. Dishonor generates losses.

HONOR: ONE OF THE FUNDAMENTALS OF THE KINGDOM OF GOD

Honor is not an option in the Kingdom of God. Honor is an obligation in the Kingdom of God. A Kingdom cannot survive with citizens practicing dishonor all the time.

Honor is part of the culture of the Kingdom. She produces a lifestyle in citizens. It has to be so natural that it doesn't get anyone's attention. When honor is lived and practiced correctly, the name of the Lord is glorified and exalted. Honor must exalt the Lord, never man.

The culture of the world is the culture of dishonor. That is why people only notice our losses, our mistakes, the negative things that are evident in us because it is easier for them to be marked by dishonor than honor.

See the theme of honor in the priesthood

> *"A son honors his father,*
> *And a servant his master.*

> If then I am the Father,
> Where is my honor?
> And if I am a Master,
> Where is My reverence?
> Says the Lord of hosts
> To you priests who despise My name.
> Yet you say, 'In what way have we despised Your name?'
> 7 *"You offer defiled food on My altar,*
> *But say,*
> *'In what way have we defiled You?'*
> *By saying,*
> *'The table of the Lord is contemptible.'*
> *8 And when you offer the blind as a sacrifice,*
> *Is it not evil?*
> *And when you offer the lame and sick,*
> *Is it not evil?*
> *Offer it then to your governor!*
> *Would he be pleased with you?*
> *Would he accept you favorably?"*
> Says the Lord of hosts.
> Malachi 1:6-8 NKJV

The issue was not the lack of the offering but the quality of it. God cannot just given anything, He is worthy of receiving an offering that honors Him. All who want to approach the Eternal must arrive with the purpose of honoring him.

Man can never impose an offering on God. The offering of honor is an offering of quality, and this quality is not according to human models but according to the divine standard.

Throughout the Bible you will see the Lord determining the quality of what pleases you.

So, it was in the Garden of Eden. Thus, in the construction of the Ark, when he dictated the construction and the measures. It was so in the construction of the Tabernacle. Both in measurements and material and even in the position of the Tabernacle. So, it was also in the functioning of the priestly work within the Tabernacle.

Even the position of the tribes around the Tabernacle was according to their will. It was like that at the entrance to Canaan. It was so in the distribution of land for the tribes.

In short, honor is in doing what the Lord determines for our lives. The disgrace is in not doing what he commands and not giving what he asks of us.
Honor is the twin sister of obedience. One does not live without the other.

DISHONOR ADVANCES ON GENERATIONS
How sin opens the doors of dishonor

DAVID'S CASE

King David is known in the Bible as a man of honor. In all the opportunities he had, he always proved to love and honor the Lord. The Lord even uttered a special word about him when he said: He is a man according to my heart.

22 And when He had removed him, He raised up for them David as king, to whom also He gave testimony and said, 'I have found David the son of Jesse, a man after My own heart, who will do all My will.'
Acts 13:22 NKJV

That is a powerful truth and in fact David, honored the Lord in all that was demanded of him.

However, what amazes us is that even a man of honor like David can open a door of dishonor in his life and be tormented by dishonor until the end of his days.

I am sure that most of the men called by God to serve at the altar, when they are ordained and initiate the fulfillment of their ministries, they have no intention of betraying or dishonoring God. It would be crazy if they thought so when they were called.

In the development of the ministry many situations occur that are beyond the control of the man of God and, if they did not have an emotional control and great conviction of his call, he can commit acts that dishonor the Lord. Even having certainty of the call, of the anointing received and putting every effort, it is necessary to keep a strict watch on your actions and decisions to avoid losing focus and dishonor your Lord.

Remember, minister of the Lord, all our work is carried out in the territory of the enemy. The apostle John warns us that this world is under the evil one.

We know that we are of God, and the whole world lies under the sway of the wicked one.
1 John 5:19 NKJV

It is in this world under the evil one that we fulfill our ministry. It is in the land of dishonor that we do our work of honor.

Bathsheba: The Door Of David's Dishonor

David fell in love with a woman named Bathsheba. She was a married woman, whose husband was at war fighting for her country and for her king.

The king saw her, wanted her and slept with her. This adultery generated a pregnancy. That was the beginning of dishonor in David's life. Let's go to the Bible:

It happened in the spring of the year, at the time when kings go out to battle, that David sent Joab and his servants with him, and all Israel; and they destroyed the people of Ammon and besieged Rabbah. But David remained at Jerusalem.
2 Then it happened one evening that David arose from his bed and walked on the roof of the king's house. And from the roof he saw a woman bathing, and the woman was very beautiful to behold.
3 So David sent and inquired about the woman. And someone said, "Is this not Bathsheba, the daughter of Eliam, the wife of Uriah the Hittite?"
4 Then David sent messengers, and took her; and she came to him, and he lay with her, for she was cleansed from her impurity; and she returned to her house.
5 And the woman conceived; so she sent and told David, and said, "I am with child."
2 Samuel 11:1-5 NKJV

David's army had defeated the Ammonites on the battlefield, and when possible he sent more troops to besiege Rabba. The Ammonites were resisting hard in Raba, their main city. Joab, the great general of David, established a siege to the city and maintained military pressure on the enemies.

Joab awaited David's arrival to conclude the attack and lead the Ammonites to final defeat.

David decided not to go to war and left everything in the hands of his commander and his troops. The king's place was the main command post of his army. David was not because he decided to stay at home.

Negligence with his responsibility and with his army placed him in a position of indulgence and idleness. Hence the sin of adultery was only a small step.

ANALYZE THE SITUATIONS THAT LEADS TO THE FIRST SIN

Relaxation in your responsibility

Instead of leading his troops, which heroic commander, honoring the position the Lord gave him, he delegated responsibility to his subordinates and stayed in Jerusalem enjoying his spare time while others fought and died for and for the kingdom.

He wanted tranquility and enjoy vacations. One afternoon he rose from his bed. Where he had enjoyed a pleasant nap instead of doing something for its construction or attending the palace business. Or he could deal with the prayers he used to practice in the afternoon.

Everything makes it seem that this day, David, had lost the focus of such a sublime spiritual exercise.

Eyes Out Of Focus

When he saw the woman, his eyes at once were out of focus of his responsibilities. His position as king was already compromised.

Adultery ends in bed but begins in the heart. The leader who departs from his essential duties of the ministry ends his thoughts where he should not.

THE STEPS OF SIN AND THE STEPS OF DISHONOR

Good desires are key to the door of honor. Bad desire is the key to the door of dishonor.

David saw her and wanted her. He sent for her even knowing she was married and slept with her.

THE DEVELOPMENT PROCESS BEGINS

First Step:

King David dishonors a marriage by sleeping with the wife of the neighbor. It transgresses one of the commandments of the Decalogue: "You will not covet your neighbor's wife."

Second Step:

David dishonors that woman's husband because he took his partner. Uriah was passionate about his wife who in turn corresponded to her husband's love. With such an attitude, David destroyed an honest home that lived in complete happiness. Adulterers never reason that their moment of carnal pleasure fills innocent people who lived in marital peace with bitterness.

Third Step:

Uriah was demoralized as a soldier. David dishonors and demoralizes a soldier who defended his kingdom. A subordinate of his who was defending him on the field of battle where David should also be leading his troops.

Fourth Step:

David dishonors his wives with whom he was married, despising them as women. They became mocked by the women who lived in the kingdom. Most likely adultery was consummated in the palace. David didn't worry about the psychological or emotional conditions of his wives. Dishonor has no limits.

Fifth Step:

David dishonors his children who now become children of an adulterous father. With this attitude, he forgot to behave as an example for them. Adultery generates deep scars in the heart of your own family. When an adult leader, it is easier to find the forgiveness of those from outside than those of his own family living with him.

Sixth Step:

David dishonors the people who he ruled over people who saw him as an example of a warrior, a strong king and a fervent worshiper of God. Now they see him as any adulterer. He lost credibility. Although he had not lost the authority of the king, because no one could remove him from his post, since it was God who established him. From now on it would be an authority exercised by the moral force of the law but not by the moral force.

Seventh Step:

David dishonors himself. He lost the posture of royalty and became a commoner who does crazy things. He left his prophetic position for the bed of bitterness. In the beginning, he did not perceive that, but as time went by and the following events, he discovered the great damage of his attitude.

ANALYZE THE SITUATIONS THAT LEAD THE SECOND SIN

King David perceived his situation and devised a plan to solve the problem. Every man far from God always thought of a plan to get out of the well in which he got into.

Eve got rid of her problem by blaming the snake. Adam, after blaming Eve for her mistake, also devised a plan and put together sheets to make a dress with which to cover her nakedness. You take advantage of the creative plans devised by a man who is far from God.

Today in Brazil, and in Latin American countries, there are many church leaders rising to the pulpit with figs made of fig leaves.
He sent for Uriah, husband of Bathsheba, to the battlefield.

The Process Of The Second Sin Begins

General Joab sent, according to the king's order, that Uriah return to Jerusalem and present himself before David. The obedient officer returned, introduced himself and was rewarded eating at the king's table, without imagining why and without distrust of anything. David didn't understand why he was so honored with him.

> *6 Then David sent to Joab, saying, "Send me Uriah the Hittite." And Joab sent Uriah to David.*
> *7 When Uriah had come to him, David asked how Joab was doing, and how the people were doing, and how the war prospered.*
> *8 And David said to Uriah, "Go down to your house and wash your feet." So Uriah departed from the king's house, and a gift of food from the king followed him.*
> *9 But Uriah slept at the door of the king's house with all the servants of his lord, and did not go down to his house.*
> *10 So when they told David, saying, "Uriah did not go down to his house," David said to Uriah, "Did you not come from a journey? Why did you not go down to your house?"*
> *11 And Uriah said to David, "The ark and Israel and Judah are dwelling in tents, and my lord Joab and the servants of my lord are encamped in the open fields.*

Shall I then go to my house to eat and drink, and to lie with my wife? As you live, and as your soul lives, I will not do this thing."
12 Then David said to Uriah, "Wait here today also, and tomorrow I will let you depart." So Uriah remained in Jerusalem that day and the next.
13 Now when David called him, he ate and drank before him; and he made him drunk. And at evening he went out to lie on his bed with the servants of his lord, but he did not go down to his house.
14 In the morning it happened that David wrote a letter to Joab and sent it by the hand of Uriah. 15 And he wrote in the letter, saying, "Set Uriah in the forefront of the hottest battle, and retreat from him, that he may be struck down and die." 2 Samuel 11:6-15 NKJV

As the first sin was not resolved, the door opened for the second Living in dishonor and without regret, man does anything to get rid of the great accusations of his own conscience. The man in sin is a prisoner of himself.

King David was about 50 years old on this occasion, he was no longer an immature young man. At this age it should necessarily have a strong character and sufficient maturity not to fall into that bond. There begins to manifest a side of his life that showed his weakness.

When he sent for Urias, he wanted to transfer his sin to Bathsheba's husband. He did not want to assume his own mistake.

Asked how Joab was, how the people and the war were going, he showed a simulation. As it is popularly said, it was nothing more than trivial conversation.

He tries to manipulate Uriah to go to sleep with his wife who had already become pregnant. Uriah, a man of honor, was not manipulated or defeated by the man of dishonor.

Seeing the failure of his plan, he tried to intoxicate Urias to manipulate it according to his plans, but he did not succeed either.

Finally, it reaches the end of its plan. Plot the death of Uriah, to stay with the widow. He writes a letter with the death sentence of Uriah, instructing him to take the letter to General Joab.

The respect, faithfulness and honor that Uriah had for his king was so great that he carried the letter without trying to open it and discover its contents along the way. David, who had committed the sin of adultery, now committed a premeditated crime.

So, now he was an adulterer and a criminal. But the process of dishonor did not stop, it continued on its way.

Eighth Step:
By sending the death letter, David disgraces himself before his army and his commanders. What military man, be he a soldier or a general, is going to trust a boss who commands his own subordinates to be killed? He broke the discipline and broke the chain of command.

Ninth Step:
David forgot a very important detail. He killed a man who was loved by his wife. Did David ever think that this marriage was happy and that he destroyed that happiness? He did not worry about destroying Bathsheba's feelings for her husband. Did David think that he would be loved by a widow whose husband he had murdered?

Dear leader, when the sinner's dishonor strikes the soul of his neighbor, the trauma lasts until his death.

As we will see, the harvest of dishonor is terrible.

THE PROPHET NATHAN ENTERS SCENE AND PUTS THINGS IN ORDER

Sin brought many pains to David. He became a weak leader and a composer without songs. "For I acknowledge my rebellions, and my sin is always before me" (Psalm 51: 1)

God in his wisdom knows how to act, and knows how to act at the right time. God waited until David's joy was exhausted to immediately enter the scene (Psalm 51:12)

Then Nathan arose. On their own? No. "And the Lord sent Nathan to David" (2 Samuel 12: 1).

Nathan was not sent after adultery. He was not sent when Bathsheba became pregnant. He was not sent when David murdered Uriah. He was not sent when the baby was born. God waited for the right moment and the right person.

Although we have thousands of things to add about David's deeds, God added one that we may never be able to grant, forgiveness and restitution.

As a good surgeon, God uses the precise tool to remove the tumor from the soul of his anointed. God knew how he was. He knows who we are, but believe him, he has the exact time and the right person to send it to us.

God did not send a religious fanatic to treat David, he sent a friend, Nathan. That he ate at his table, participated in his life and that he cared for the kingdom and for God who ruled it. He was one of the prophets of the Kingdom.

With great grace Nathan pronounced the right words and had a graceful attitude. His wisdom caused David to wake up and see the seriousness of his mistake. Nathan did not use dishonorable and humiliating criticism, but he illustrated the fact so admirably that David had no choice but to bend his knees and thank God for the correction.

Nathan was the doctor, and at the same time the surgical instrument of the operation. That is what God expects of us. That instead of criticisms that solve little, we can cure our generation with the word of wisdom.

Nathan created a parable and told it to David who did not perceive it was his situation. After all, a year after his adultery had passed, the boy was born. David "forgot" his sin. God sent the prophet to remember him.

When David acknowledged his mistake, Nathan let go of the prophetic word about him and talked about what the harvest would be like for all the dishonor:

7 Then Nathan said to David, "You are the man! Thus says the Lord God of Israel: 'I anointed you king over Israel, and I delivered you from the hand of Saul.
8 I gave you your master's house and your master's wives into your keeping, and gave you the house of Israel and Judah. And if that had been too little, I also would have given you much more!
9 Why have you despised the commandment of the Lord, to do evil in His sight? You have killed Uriah the Hittite with the sword; you have taken his wife to be your wife, and have killed him with the sword of the people of Ammon.
10 Now therefore, the sword shall never depart from your house, because you have despised Me, and have taken the wife of Uriah the Hittite to be your wife.'
11 Thus says the Lord: 'Behold, I will raise up adversity against you from your own house; and I will take your wives before your eyes and give them to your neighbor, and he shall lie with your wives in the sight of this sun.
12 For you did it secretly, but I will do this thing before all Israel, before the sun.'"
2 Samuel 12:7-12 NKJV

David did not wait for Nathan to finish the prophecy and opened his mouth and showed his repentance: "I sinned against the Lord"

With repentance came forgiveness. And Nathan completed the prophecy:

13 So David said to Nathan, "I have sinned against the Lord." And Nathan said to David, "The Lord also has put away your sin; you shall not die.
14 However, because by this deed you have given great occasion to the enemies of the Lord to blaspheme, the child also who is born to you shall surely die."
2 Samuel 12:13-14 NKJV

Sin was forgiven. God loved David and was not going to lose him in any way. But there was the matter of dishonor. David would have a tragic harvest in his family's history.

He dishonored a family. And dishonor entered his family, leading them to moments of frustration and sadness with the events within their lineage. It was the harvest.

Episodes Of Dishonor In David's Life

See the acts of dishonor that marked the life of this great king

a. The child dies, the fruit of adultery: 2 Samuel 12:18
   The wages of sin: Romans 6:23
b. The shame of incest in the family between their children Tamar and Amnon: 2 Samuel 13: 1-22
   It reminded him of the sin he sowed.
c. The death of Amnon came, commanded by his own brother Absalom, to bring to mind the death of Uriah: 2 Samuel 13: 28-29
d. A usurper of the throne appears in the person of his own son Absalom, to remind him that he used the place of Uriah: 2 Samuel 15: 1-18
e. Sexual dishonor explodes over his home when Absalom cohabited with his concubines in public, to remind him of what he did in secret to Uriah's wife: 2 Samuel 16: 21-22
f. The treacherous death of Absalom arrived, to remind him of the treacherous death he made with Uriah: 2 Samuel 18: 12-15
g. God sent the plague, to remind him of his pride and make him humble: 2 Samuel 24: 10-17

Let's go back to the beginning of everything. All these things were fruits caused by a night of love with the wrong woman. With the woman of dishonor. With a woman who loved her husband. All this because of an act of dishonor. It was nothing more than adultery. It was a storm of dishonor.

The harvest of dishonor came in the form of a tsunami. It devastated everything. David changed a night of pleasure for 20 years of tragedy. Is that worth it?

Adultery is never just adultery. It is truly the door of dishonor that opens and is wide open, tormenting day and night.

THE LEADER AND DISHONOR

When They "Steal Our Sheep"

The punishment of dishonor is sometimes imperceptible. Sometimes who is going through a process of those, does not notice why the events that occur in his ministry and his life.

A pastor from another ministry takes one of its main members. The one who had always been faithful and who had been the best tithe. As dishonor is imperceptible, you do not notice that there is an open door of dishonor and someone entered through that door, went to your flock and stole your blessing.

Where Are The Finances Of The Ministry?

The finances of his ministry do not grow. You teach, minister, pray, do prophetic act and the money disappears. So many people working in their church but do not tithe, do not offer and do not give first fruits. He has a door of dishonor open.

Have you honored your leader with your tithes and first fruits? If you are not doing so, how do you expect your members to tithe and give first fruits in your life? Close that door. The sooner you close it, the faster the blessings will return to your life.

If not you will be singing the song of the defeated: "the people are hard to please." "The people of this church are miserable." "My church is in blessing, we only have a problem in the financial area." "The people only want blessings." "The people don't know how to honor me."

Wake up leader. Look in the mirror. Preach for yourself. Then start closing the doors of dishonor.

Dishonor attracts scarcity.

Why are there so many leaders with extraordinary ministerial capacity, great apostles, prophets, teachers, pastors and evangelists, as well as other ministries and gifts going through moments of such deprivation that they cannot even testify to the greatness of God?

They know how to teach, minister, pray, prophesy, shepherd others, but they don't do it with themselves. They want honor, much honor.

But who are they honoring? Will honor be a lifestyle for them? The wise men of God give honor. Foolish children seek honor. Those who honor will always be honored. But those who dishonor will always be dishonored.

> *30 Therefore the Lord God of Israel says: 'I said indeed that your house and the house of your father would walk before Me forever.' But now the Lord says: 'Far be it from Me; for those who honor Me I will honor, and those who despise Me shall be lightly esteemed.*
> *1 Samuel 2:30 NKJV*

This word was uttered to one of the great high priests and judges of Israel. A man who did an extraordinary job. He was also a great prophet, as well as a disciple of another great prophet and judge like Samuel.

Until the day he let dishonor into his priesthood, through his children. Surely you already know quite well the story of Eli and that of his children Phinehas and Hophni.

CLOSE THAT DOOR. BECOME A MAN OF HONOR

The only way for you to permanently close the doors of dishonor in your life and in your ministry is to learn to live in honor and honor your neighbor. When you honor someone, you are honoring God.

The determination to live in honor started from him, because honor is one of the foundations of the Kingdom.

God places the seed of honor in every place and in every person. You just need to grow it.

1. Rahab lived in prostitution (dishonor) but had the seed of honor and knew how to cultivate it.
2. Eli had the dishonor in his house: Phinehas and Hophni. But he also had the seed of honor: Samuel.
3. David dishonored. But he was a man who had the seed within himself. He was a man according to the heart of God.
4. Noah had three children. One was dishonorable. The other two were of honor.

5. Ruth was a Moabite, a people without honor, but she was a woman of honor and honored Naomi and was honored in Israel.
6. Jonathan was the son of a father without honor: Saul. But Jonathan honored David, recognizing him as the future king of Israel. Charge that by law should belong to Jonathan.
7. David honored Jonathan even after he died when he rescued, protected and enriched his disabled son Mefiboset. He rescued him from Lodebar.
8. King Jehu commanded Jezabel to be buried, because she was of royal lineage and was entitled to funeral funerals of the king. She did not deserve that, but Jehu could not renounce his position as king because of her.

Then he said, "Throw her down." So they threw her down, and some of her blood spattered on the wall and on the horses; and he trampled her underfoot.
34 And when he had gone in, he ate and drank. Then he said, "Go now, see to this accursed woman, and bury her, for she was a king's daughter."
2 Kings 9:33-34 NKJV

You can continue to search the Bible and you will find hundreds of cases of honor. The word of God is a book of honor. Honor is foundation, so it appears throughout the Bible.

Living in honor, you will surely be enjoying your prophetic position. The position for which God called and positioned him. All men and women who discovered honor in the Bible took possession of their prophetic destiny.

Today there are people suffering and accusing the devil for their sufferings. They do not understand that the problem is within them.

There are Christians who made the mistake of dishonoring their leaders and today, even if they go from church to church, they continue to suffer the consequences of having dishonored those who had authority over their lives. They are sowing the wrong seed.

Redo your covenant with God. Like David, abandon dishonor and honor your lifestyle, and use it as an instrument of victory in all areas of your life.

And God, our God will always honor you. Be blessed and blessed.

About The Author

Paulo Ventura is a writer, international speaker, and leader of the Kingdom Conquerors Apostolic Network. He earned a bachelor's degree in Theology from the Pentecostal Bible Institute in Rio de Janeiro. He completed his master's degree at Shalom Bible College and Seminary in Pennsylvania, USA. And a doctorate in Canada from a Christian College.

He graduated as a Civil Diplomat and International Chaplain from Jethro International Chaplaincy, integrated with Full Revival Church in Massachusetts, and is accredited to serve as a chaplain at the International Red Cross with 154 countries.

Married to the apostle Cosma Ventura, the apostle Paul Ventura has four daughters, all working in the ministry.

Exercising his ministry inside and outside Brazil, for more than 46 uninterrupted years, the apostle Paul has been at the forefront of many projects and evangelistic actions.

His next project, of international scope that is already underway, is the creation and establishment of the Theological University of the Kingdom. Whose bases are already laid in the United States, by his apostle daughter Marcia Aviles.

BIBLIOGRAPHY

Bibles Consulted:

Almeida - João Ferreira de Almeida – Revista e atualizada

Reina – Valera – Edición 1960

King James – 1611

Edição Vida Nova – 1960

Bíblia de Referência Thompson – 1988

Bíblia Hebraica – David Gorodovits e Jairo Fridlin - Ed Sefer

Bíblia Peshita – Edición Española – Traducción de los Antiguos Manuscritos Arameus. Edição 2006 – Instituto Cultural Álef e Tau.

Almeida – Edição Contemporânea – Editora Vida – 1990

Other Publications:

1. O Novo Testamento Interpretado – 6 volumes. Russell Norman Champlin. Editora Milenium.

2. Enciclopédia de Bíblia – Teologia e Filosofia – 6 volumes. Edição 1995 - Russell Norman Champlin. Editora e Distribuidora Candeia

3. Comentário Judaico do Novo Testamento – David H. Stern – Edição 2007 – Editora Atos.

4. The New Complete Works of Josephus – Edição Revisada e Expandida – Edição 1999 – Kregel Publications.

5. Comentário al Texto Hebreo Del Antiguo Testamento – Pentateuco e Históricos – Edição Espanhola 2008 – Volume 1 – Keil e Delitzsch – Editorial Clie

6. Dicionário Internacional de Teologia do Antigo Testamento – R. Laird Harris – Gleason L. Archer Jr – Bruce K. Waltke – 1ª Edição 1998 – Sociedade Religiosa Edições Vida Nova.

NOTES

Made in the USA
Columbia, SC
26 April 2025